DEDICATION and LEADERSHIP

DOUGLAS HYDE

DEDICATION

and

LEADERSHIP

Learning from the Communists

University of Notre Dame Press

Published in the United States in 1966
by University of Notre Dame Press
Notre Dame, Indiana 46556

Second printing   1969
Third printing   1970
Fourth printing   1971
Fifth printing   1974
Sixth printing   1976
Seventh printing 1977
Eighth printing   1980

Library of Congress Catalog Number: 66-19032

Printed in the United States of America

Preface

THE origin and evolution of this book need to be understood if its purpose is not to be misunderstood. It began as an attempt to answer from my own experience the question which is so often asked: 'Why are Communists so dedicated and successful as leaders whilst others so often are not?'

I was asked to try to answer this in a series of lectures given as a Leadership Training Seminar at the annual convention of the Mission Secretariat in Washington, D.C. Present were hundreds of religious and lay leaders who had come from almost every part of the world, but particularly from Asia, Africa and Latin America.

The sponsors urged me to talk as freely as I wished, since the purpose was to examine where Catholics were weak and, by contrast, where the Communists were strong. I took them at their word and pulled no punches. This explains why, throughout this book—in which I have retained the form of the spoken rather than the written word—I stress Communist successes and Catholic weaknesses.

The original seminar was in due course adapted to the needs of other organisations, religious and non-religious. It is my hope that in its present form *Dedication and Leadership* may have something new to offer the politician, the man who is interested in the psychology of Communism and, in particular, the man who believes that there is an urgent need for leadership at every level in the non-Communist world. For, above all, this book is intended as a challenge.

Douglas Hyde

Contents

CHAPTER I

The Starting Point

THERE are two points it is necessary to make, right at the start, so that we may have the aim and purpose of this study clear. Firstly, the subject is dedication and leadership, not anti-Communism. Secondly, we shall in the main be discussing those Communist leadership training methods which are capable of imitation or adaptation by Christians and others or, conversely, which may spark off some useful and constructive thought about our own methods.

If in the process we arrive at a better understanding of the motivation and formation of the Communist cadres, then so much the better. Indeed, I hope that this may be a useful by-product of this discussion. But its main purpose is to see what we can learn from the Communists' attitudes, methods and techniques.

We shall be looking at the Communists, not in order to attack, not to prove them wrong, but rather to see what they have to teach us. So when I describe Communist methods I shall not select those which have nothing for us. Quite obviously I shall not be recommending those which, for moral or ethical reasons, we must abhor, although even here we may in fact find that some of these still merit examination, even if only because of the single-minded approach the Communists bring to them. This will be a highly selective look at the Communists and Communism.

Even the examples I quote will be the best I have seen after years of living with Communists and observing Communism in almost every part of the world.

When I left Communism after twenty years in the Party, I knew its evils. But I also believed that the Communists were right in some important respects. For example, when they said that there is a great battle going on all over the world which in the final analysis is a struggle for men's hearts, minds and souls. We can accept this even if we do not take the view that all the 'goodies' are on one side and the 'baddies' are on the other. There is plenty of evidence that the thought of millions today is in a state of flux, people everywhere are breaking away from age-old allegiances, beliefs and ways of life, and it is much too early yet to say where the process will finish.

I believe that they are right, too, when they say that, although we may not see the end of the battle, its outcome will most probably be decided in this period in which we are living. In short, this is a turning-point in man's history, a terrible, yet tremendous time in which to live.

This has, of course, been said before by other generations. In the past, however, when men talked of the fate of 'the whole world' and 'all mankind' being at stake they could mean only a small part of the surface of the globe, the one in which lived only a minority of the human race. When we talk of a world-wide battle today we mean one which involves men in every country everywhere.

When, therefore, the Communists speak of launching the world on the way to Communism in the period in which we are living, it is this that they mean—not the whole world with the exception of the United States, or the United Kingdom or whichever country, being your own, you may feel is proof against assault.

10

Their aim is quite clear. They have never concealed it and it is something that is immensely meaningful to every Communist. It is a Communist world. In the past half-century they have achieved one-third of that aim. On any reckoning, that is a remarkable achievement, probably an unprecedented one. Nonetheless the world in which we live is still predominantly non-Communist. Twice as many people live in the non-Communist world as live under Communism. There is no basis here for defeatism.

Even so, it is probably true to say of the Communists that never in man's history has a small group of people set out to win a world and achieved more in less time. Certainly, they have brought far more people under their sway by the methods they employ than anyone else has done during the same period. Moreover, they have always worked through a minority. This is true of those territories which they now rule and also of those where they have not yet come to power.

This is, however, less exceptional than would appear. In practice, most organisations and causes work through minorities. Even those who believe most deeply in majority rule still depend upon the faithful few to do the work, to make the necessary sacrifices in time, energy and devotion to keep the movement going.

The Communists have learned from experience, and as a result both of pooling their ideas and of learning from the successes and failures of their movement everywhere, how best they can make the maximum impact upon others, even though they must work through a minority. Many of the methods they have evolved have grown out of this realisation. It is these that I consider it is most useful for us to examine.

The Communist Party throughout the world has thirty-six million members. Of these, a very high proportion live in lands ruled by Communism. There, quite consciously

11

and deliberately the party is kept small so that it may retain the character of an élite. Only a few million live and work in the non-Communist world. Yet the impact they make upon it is such that we are conscious of their presence the whole of the time. They have profoundly influenced the thought of the majority. The policies of other parties are notably different from what they would otherwise have been because the Communists exist.

Communists are a very small minority, in comparison with some of the other groups who are also contending for men's hearts and minds. There are, for example, 400 million Moslems and more than 500 million Catholics, the majority of whom live outside the Communist countries. These other great world movements have immensely larger human resources at their disposal than have the combined Communist parties. Yet no one could claim that in the period in which Communism has been in our midst they have had anything like its success. I am not, of course, talking of their ability to seize power by force of arms or by subterfuge, but of their ability to fire the imagination, create a sense of dedication and send their followers into effective, meaningful action.

It is almost impossible to read a newspaper or to listen to the news on radio or television without learning of something which the Communists are doing. They never let us forget them. This is not just an accident, there are reasons for it and these are worth examining.

I do not believe that the strength of Communism lies in the strength of its ideas. I believe, as any Christian must, that Christianity has something infinitely better to offer than has Communism. To put it in the rather degraded terminology of our times, we have something immensely better to sell. Yet it is they who have been able to influence our generation much more profoundly than have we.

Beliefs are important to Communists. Communist poli-

12

cies grow out of them. Reading Marx, Engels, Lenin, may not be easy but it is necessary to an understanding of Communists and Communism. But it is not this that attracts people to the Communist cause. In my experience, the strength of Communism lies in its people and the way in which they are used. It is at this level that Communists have most to teach us. They use well the human material at their disposal. Most often non-Communists do not.

Perhaps I should make it clear that when I speak of Communists in these terms I do so against a background of having associated with Communists in almost every part of the world, not just some special sort of British Communists, or Western Communists, who live in affluent societies. A point which must be grasped in any discussion of world Communism is that Communists are, or become, much of a type the world over. They have certain things in common which distinguish them everywhere.

For twenty years I was a member of the British Communist Party. I joined when I was seventeen years of age. I spent all my late adolescence and early manhood in the Party. By the time I left it, almost every friend I had in the world was a Communist. Communism had been my life and I could claim to know Communists, or at any rate the Communists of Britain, very well. Normally, the ex-Communist, particularly one who has come out publicly and so is dubbed as a renegade, is cut off from his old comrades and from the movement with which he has been associated.

It happens that since I left the Party a steady stream of Communists has been in touch with me. With the exception of the first few months after my resignation from the Party and its daily paper, of which I was news editor, there has been no period when I was not in touch with some, at least, of the Party's members. I did not in the first instance seek them out. They had heard what I said in public lectures, or they had read what I had written about them in books and articles; they recognised that I was trying to give a faithful picture of them as they really were; and so, when they were in any difficulty or began to feel any doubt about their communism, some of them turned to me, believing that I would understand. The result has been a living 'dialogue' which has continued over the years.

As a commentator on world affairs, I have travelled in almost every area of the world. Wherever I have gone, I have continued to keep in touch with Communists and Communism. Since 1957 I have spent several months of each year living in prison cells with Asian Communist leaders who were serving prison sentences after having led jungle wars or insurrections, or who were detainees in lands where Communism was banned and the Party an illegal, clandestine organisation. What I have to say, therefore, about the Communists' use of people relates to members of many different races, in many different parts of the world.

Again, in order to get the picture clear, it must be noted that the human material on which they work is not something different from that which is at the disposal of others. The majority of Communists are 'first generation'. This means that others, frequently Christians and Christian missionaries, had them in their hands long before they went to the Communist Party. One can, and must for honesty's sake, be more specific: often these people are identical with those who are available to Christians to instruct and use in the sense that a disturbingly high proportion of them, particularly those who form the hard core of the Communist Party, were once Catholics. In other words the Communists train and use successfully people with whom Christians had failed. I am not just theorising: any analysis of the origins of the leadership of the Communist Party of, say, Britain, U.S.A., Australia

14

or, for that matter, Kerala (South India), will provide ample evidence of the Communist ability to attract to their ranks lapsed and fallen-away Catholics.

I make this point, which may seem a brutal one, for two reasons: first, it is necessary to appreciate that there is no basis for the belief that Communists have some special sort of human material on which to work. The people with whom they frequently have great success are our own failures. Secondly, we must in humility accept that amongst the Christians, and Catholics in particular, who go to the Communists are many who find in Communism what they had hoped, without success, to find among the Christians. The onus is, therefore, on us to find the answer to this problem.

If we recognise that Communists are not some different brand of human beings from those who make up other, comparable movements, we must then turn to their methods and see what part these play in assisting the Communist Party to develop its members' potentialities for dedication and leadership.

The Christian who is trying to train and produce leaders may object that Christians are concerned with the super-natural and must operate at that level, whereas Communists are concerned only with the natural. I would sub-mit that this is not a reason for ignoring the natural. It is theologically sound to say that the supernatural is built on the natural. In considering the Communists' methods we shall be dealing with the question at the natural level which is precisely where the Christian tends often to be at his weakest. It is here that we have most to learn.

Willingness to Sacrifice

If you ask me what is the distinguishing mark of the Communist, what it is that Communists most outstandingly have in common, I would not say, as some people might expect, their ability to hate—this is by no means common to them all. I would say that beyond any shadow of doubt it is their idealism, their zeal, dedication, devotion to their cause and willingness to sacrifice. This characterises the Communists wherever Communism has still to come to power and is obviously true of many in the very different circumstances where it now rules. The vast majority of the Communists I have met anywhere conform to this pattern.

This is no accident. It does not just happen. The Communists have evolved their own means by which they are able to evoke an exceptional degree of dedication. And they use it very effectively indeed. To understand how it is done, one must follow through the process step by step from the start.

The majority of those who join the Communist Party are young. The average joining age used to be between seventeen and twenty-five. Today it is between fifteen and twenty-five. For some years now they have been recruiting successfully among fifteen to seventeen-year-olds. The British Communist Party recently organised a recruiting campaign which brought in several thousand new members. When, in due course, the General Secretary made his report to the Executive Committee, he said that most of those who joined during the period of the campaign were between the ages of fifteen and nineteen.

A majority of the Asian Communists with whom I have shared prison cells joined the movement when they were at school. Go to Caracas, Venezuela, and you will find that some of the Communists' greatest successes are amongst high school and secondary school boys and girls. Some of the guerilla bands in the mountains of Venezuela are manned almost exclusively by youngsters of this age who have left their homes and their studies in order to be

16

able to start the armed fight for Communism. The first sign of Communism which missionaries in Africa have discovered has often been when strikes occurred in their own mission schools. In other words, the successful appeal to the very young is not a British phenomenon. One finds it everywhere.

Youth is a period of idealism. The Communists attract young people by appealing directly to that idealism. Too often, others have failed either to appeal to it or to use it and they are the losers as a consequence. We have no cause to complain if, having neglected the idealism of youth, we see others come along, take it, use it and harness it to their cause—and against our own.

It is fashionable in some circles today to sneer at 'starry-eyed idealism'. Of all the ways of helping Communism I can think of none better than this. That sort of cynicism has driven many eager, earnest, intelligent and potentially good youngsters to believe that the West has nothing to offer the young idealist but cynicism, and that this is an expression of the decadence of our way of life. It has led them to believe that if you are interested in improving man's lot on earth, if you want to change the world (and the boy who does not want to do this at some point during his adolescence will certainly make a cynical old materialist later on), it is to the Communists, not to the Christians, you must turn.

Wherever I have travelled I have found that young people are idealistic. This is natural to any healthy youngster. I can only conclude that it is the way God wants them to be. We offend against charity and justice, and against commonsense too, when we sneer at starry-eyed idealism. We do it to our own loss.

Young people have always dreamed of better worlds and we must hope that they always will. The day we lose our dreams all progress will cease. Idealistic young people will want to change the world and will pursue their own idealistic course in any case. If their idealism is not appealed to and canalised within the circles in which they have grown up they will seek elsewhere for an outlet.

The Communists have demonstrated that the idealism of youth is something which can be harnessed and used with tremendous effect. It is a dynamic thing. Despite all the twists and turns of Communist policy it continues over the years to provide the dynamism of the Communist movement.

Older Christians, believing that you cannot build perfect worlds and perfect societies from fallen men, too often take up what is at best a superciliously tolerant approach to youthful idealism—when they do not ignore it altogether. The Communists take it and use it.

Communism becomes the dominant thing in the life of the Communist. It is something to which he gives himself completely. Quite obviously it meets a need, fills a vacuum at the time when he is first attracted to it. More significant is that it normally continues to be the dominant force in the life of the Communist for as long as he remains in the movement.

The Communists' appeal to idealism is direct and audacious. They say that if you make mean little demands upon people, you will get a mean little response which is all you deserve, but, if you make big demands on them, you will get an heroic response. They prove in practice that this is so, over and over again. They work on the assumption that if you call for big sacrifices people will respond to this and, moreover, the relatively smaller sacrifices will come quite naturally.

When I first went to work on the British Communist Party's daily paper, I was proud that I had been chosen for the work, proud to make whatever sacrifice was asked of me, but I was nonetheless conscious of the fact that I had willingly accepted a ludicrously small wage. I will admit that I felt slightly virtuous about this—until I met other members of the staff. Most of them were older than I was at that time, they had gone further in their careers (and some had gone very far indeed) and had had to make far bigger sacrifices than I. Some of them were earning one-tenth of what had been their salary when they had worked for the 'capitalist' press. There were times when, small as our salaries were, these could not be paid at all.

Even when the paper became slightly more prosperous and the staff were technically given the union rate for the job, the sacrifices still continued. We got our pay packets, opened them and immediately gave eight fourteenths of their contents to the Party and the paper—before it burned our fingers. Since everyone did this, it became something of a meaningless ritual after a while and so we did not bother even to receive the cash, it just went direct to the cause. And so it continues to this day.

Among the Party's leaders are many very able men, some of whom could command very high salaries if they were in industry or commerce. Instead, they accept the wage of a moderately-paid, skilled artisan.

This is not some peculiarity of the British Communist Party. The same is true of others. The French Communist Party, for example, was confronted with a financial crisis as a consequence of General de Gaulle's coming to power. Overnight the Party lost almost the whole of its large parliamentary group. They, like Communist Members of Parliament in Britain—when there were any—and elsewhere, had received their salaries from the State in the usual way and then, as is also the usual way with Communist M.P.s, passed them direct to the Party, who in return paid them an artisan's wage. The sudden loss of so many Deputies and their salaries led to the closing down of many a Communist Party local headquarters.

On the other side of the world, in Kuching, Sarawak, Borneo, recently a security chief mentioned to me almost with awe the case of a young man who had gone to join the underground Communist organisation. He came of a well-to-do Chinese family. His father had had no idea that he was in any way associated with the Communists until one day he disappeared. In due course the father learned that his son had gone to work as a rubber tapper for a few cents a day in a 'mixed' area. That is to say, it was one in which poor rural Chinese and Dyaks lived in close proximity to each other even though they hardly ever mixed. Above all else Sarawak's Communist organisation, which is exclusively Chinese, wants to gain a following among the indigenous people. Its leaders had called for volunteers to go and live among the Dyaks in their longhouses. The Chinese find the Dyaks' food unpalatable and practically uneatable; the lack of sanitation and regard for personal hygiene appals the Chinese. Most of the volunteers soon go down sick, but there are others who come forward to take their places, as this boy had done.

Such sacrifices, whether at the level of leaders or of rank and file, are impressive. And they do impress those who associate with the movement. Particularly impressive is the fact that sacrifice is found at all levels of the organisation. Youngsters of every continent have responded to this example of idealism expressing itself in terms of sacrifice. This is true of the newly-developing areas. It is true also of the 'decadent' West. Indeed, the more materialistic our society becomes, the more the dedicated man stands out by way of contrast. The dedicated man makes his own appeal simply by virtue of the fact that he is dedicated.

Like attracts like. Those who are attracted by the dedication they see within the movement will themselves be possessed of a latent idealism, a capacity for dedication. Thus dedication perpetuates itself. It sets the tone and pace of the movement as a whole. This being so, the movement can make big demands upon its followers, knowing that the response will come. If the majority of members of an organisation are half-hearted and largely inactive, then it is not surprising if others who join it soon conform to the general pattern. If the organisation makes relatively few demands upon its members and if they quite obviously feel under no obligation to give a very great deal to it, then those who join may be forgiven for supposing that this is the norm and that this is what membership entails.

If, on the other hand, the majority of members, from the leaders down, are characterised by their single-minded devotion to the cause, if it is quite clear that the majority are giving until it hurts, putting their time, money, thought and if necessary life itself at its disposal, then those who consider joining will assume that this is what will be expected of them. If they nonetheless make the decision to join, they will come already conditioned to sacrifice till it hurts.

It is ludicrous to suppose that half-hearted Christians can conduct a fruitful dialogue with fully-dedicated Communists. Perhaps it it this which underlies the fear of any such dialogue, felt by some Christians. They take it for granted that in any such dialogue the Communists must come out on top, that the Marxists will be the gainers, the Christians the losers. I would suggest that if this happens it will have less to do with Communist duplicity than with Communist dedication—although the Christian in such circumstances must be prepared for the duplicity too. The well-instructed, fully committed, totally dedicated Christian has little to fear. But dedication must be met with dedication. Ideally it should be backed by a genuine understanding of one's own beliefs and of the other man's

21

too. This must be the starting point for any dialogue with the Communists.

Among ex-Communists I have met have been some who, having given their all to Communism, became in time disillusioned or saw the flaws in its thinking and then, having left it, found some other cause to which they could dedicate themselves. I have sometimes been able to help this process. There are others, however, who lose their Communism but find nothing else to replace it. They are frequently rather pathetic figures. They remind me of a squeezed-out lemon. Everything has gone except traces of the old acid. They are left with nothing but disillusionment which may easily turn to cynicism. Or, even as they get on with living life as so many others live it—without any deeply held beliefs of any sort—they look back wistfully from time to time to the days when they had something to live by and for.

I was talking to such a man on one occasion. Our conversation brought back very vividly to my own mind the extent of the dedication which had been common in the Party in the days when we were both Communists together.

Often, ex-Communists meeting together can talk of the 'old days when we were in the Party' rather like old soldiers discussing nostalgically the campaigns they shared in the past. We had been doing this. We had talked of old comrades who now saw themselves as our enemies, of the campaigns in which we had engaged together.

Then, very wistfully he said: 'Do you remember what life was really like in the Party? You got up in the morning and as you shaved you were thinking of the jobs you would do for Communism that day. You went down to breakfast and read the *Daily Worker* to get the Party line —to get the shot and shell for a fight in which you were already involved. You read every item in the paper wondering how you might be able to use it for the cause.

22

'I had never been interested in sport but I read the sports pages in order to be able to discuss sport with others and to be able to say to them, "Have you read this in the *Daily Worker*?" I would follow this through by giving them the paper in the hope that they might turn from the sports pages and read the political ones too.

'On the bus or train, on my way to work, I read the *Daily Worker* as ostentatiously as I could, holding it up so that others might read the headlines and perhaps be influenced by them. I took two copies of the paper with me; the second one I left on the seat in the hope that someone would pick it up and read it.

'When I got to work, I kept the *Daily Worker* circulating. One worker after another would take it outside, read it for a few minutes and bring it back to me again. At lunchtime, in the canteen or the restaurant, I would try to start conversations with those with whom I was eating. I made a practice of sitting with different groups in order to spread my influence as widely as I could. I did not thrust Communism down their throats but steered our conversations in such a way that they could be brought round to politics or, if possible, to the campaigns which the Party was conducting at the time.

'Before I left my place of work at night, there was a quick meeting of the factory group or cell. There we discussed in a few minutes the successes and failures of the day. And we discussed, too, what we hoped to be able to do on the following day.

'I dashed home, had a quick meal and then went out, maybe to attend classes, maybe to be a tutor, maybe to join some Communist campaign, going from door to door canvassing or standing at the side of the road selling Communist papers—doing something for Communism. And I went home at night and dreamed of the jobs I was going to do for Communism the next day.'

Rather sadly he added: 'You know, life had some meaning and some purpose in those days. Life was good in the Communist Party.'

He was right. Of course it was. It is quite wrong to suppose that it is only the saints who are not sad. Sinners can get quite a lot of fun out of life too. And those who are dedicated get immensely more out of life than those who are not. The day he had described had been my life and that of most of my old comrades. It was a day in the life of a dedicated man, a normal day in the life of a hard-core Communist Party member. It is not surprising that he looked back at that life from the wasteland of his present purposeless existence with a considerable degree of nostalgia.

Perhaps I should add in passing that this was not some unthinking, uneducated man who had lived simply on his emotions and on action. He was a highly intelligent, Oxford University graduate, the very practical and down-to-earth product of a well-known political family. I make this point in order to reiterate and to emphasise as strongly as I can that it is quite erroneous to suppose that Communism appeals only to some particular type or class or race. Within the Communist Party you will find people of every type and class. And within the world Communist movement you will find people of every race. Discuss their case histories with them, probe into what first attracted them to Communism and invariably you will find that it was not Communist theories, policies or campaigns—important as these may be in the making of Communists—but the impact made upon them by some dedicated Communist which predisposed and conditioned them to associate with a movement and to accept a doctrine which would otherwise most probably have been unacceptable to them.

Let me illustrate my point from my own experience in

Asian jails. During the course of one particular year, I was in prison with six Communist leaders of three different races. One came from a feudal aristocratic background and had at one time been a University lecturer. The next was a teacher. The third had been in charge of a plantation, with a couple of hundred workers employed under him. The fourth, who came from a very poor background, had been in government service; the last two were young scientists both of whom were from business families. Six Asian Communist leaders from three different races and from almost as many classes as exist in their country. As people, they were of widely different types. No one by any stretch of ingenuity could put them into a single category, except, of course, that all had become Communists. Each had responded to the Communist appeal and in every case it was association with the Communists as people, not a prior study of Communist theory, which had prompted them. Each, too, had been prepared to risk his liberty and his career for the cause. The risk was real. I met them all in prison.

There is no mystery about the indisputable fact that Communists exert an influence out of all proportion to their numbers, once one grasps the point that practically every party member is a dedicated man in whose life, from the time he rises in the morning till the time he goes to bed at night, for 365 days of the year, Communism is the dominant force. They are helped immensely by bad social and economic conditions, by racial and social injustice, by all the imperfections of our modern society. Political situations often play straight into their hands. So, too, if we are going to be honest, do the Communists' opponents.

What distinguishes the Communist movement from most others and makes it possible for so small a minority to make so great an impact upon our time is the dedication of the average individual member and the immense and dynamic force this represents when all those individuals collectively make their contribution to the cause. Without that they would not be prepared to accept the organisation, the discipline, the unending 'Marxist education', the incessant appeals for ever more action. All these contribute to the Communist impact, but the starting point is dedication.

The Communists themselves fully appreciate this. Any Communist tutor conducting a course in leadership would insist right at the start that the very foundation and starting point must be dedication.

This is something for others who are concerned with producing leaders to appreciate too. It is of course quite possible to produce leaders of some sort by teaching certain techniques. These are not the sort of leaders the Communists are interested in, nor, I suggest, are they the ones the Christian cause requires most today. You can learn certain techniques and so become a leader who leads for himself—if by leadership you simply mean getting to the top whether it be of an organisation, a business, a profession or the political system. But the first requirement, if you are going to produce a leader for a cause, is that he should be dedicated.

CHAPTER II

Taking the Plunge

THE Communists make far bigger demands upon their people than the average Christian organisation would ever dare to make. As I have already noted, they believe that if you make big demands upon people you will get a big response. So this is made a deliberate policy on their part. They never make the small demand if they can make the big one. Contrary to what is often believed by those who have never been Communists, they do not, at any rate in non-Communist countries, normally achieve this by putting a gun, either real or metaphorical, at the member's head. This would not achieve its purpose. Dedication and willingness to sacrifice must be developed within a person, then drawn out of them, not forced in. The Communists have had to find ways and means of doing this. In the process, they have discovered that it is good psychology to ask for a lot. It is bad psychology and bad politics to ask for too little.

This is one of very many paradoxes which must face anyone who begins to delve into this aspect of Communism. Communism, we are told, is the great enemy of the individual. Under Communism in practice the human personality would be suppressed. Philosophically this is assuredly true. But in practice, whilst the Communist movement is still only as yet on the path to Communism and therefore must work through minorities and use each member to the uttermost, it shows a quite exceptional con-concern for drawing out the potentialities of every individual who comes within its discipline. The unfolding and growth of the personality of the recruit to Communism is frequently spectacular. This applies to the most diverse types.

I recall a conversation with a judge in South East Asia before whom hundreds of captured and surrendered guerilla fighters and detainees had appeared. He told me, that without prompting, he could invariably distinguish between those who were trained Communist Party members and those who were mere sympathisers. Of many of the intellectuals who came to Communism in the West in the 1930s it might be said that their association with the Communist movement led to a flowering of their talents. The finest period of many of the artists, writers and poets, who came to Communism—even though they subsequently left it—was the one when they were Communists. This was partly because their work became more meaningful to them because they now had a cause for which to live and to which they could harness their talents. But it was also the case that Communism demanded everything of them. It asked for the whole man and got it.

The paradox, I repeat, is that the Communists show a faith in their people which Christians, who are supposed to be the great defenders of the human person, are too often not prepared to show. They ask for a lot and they get the big response they expect.

At the same time, they are hard-headed enough to know that it is not sufficient to have an organisation of enthusiasts. Sacrifice, dedication and zeal are not enough in themselves. These are important, but they are only a starting-point. They are what helps to make a man persist as an active member and they ensure that when he is made a leader he continues to lead for the cause and not for himself. To achieve this you must create the initial willingness to sacrifice, but you must follow through with preparation, training and instruction as well.

So the Communists set about trying to use just as effectively as they can the human material which is at their disposal. 'Every Communist a leader, every factory a fortress' is one of their slogans. But it is more than a slogan, it is an aim, and one which they set out very determinedly to achieve. The meaning behind the slogan is this: each party member must be so trained that no matter where he may find himself he will be qualified to come forward and lead; and, when you have sufficient such members together in a given factory or within some particular organisation, they can make this a 'fortress' for Communism. In other words, their position can be made well nigh unassailable.

That this is not just a slogan is something known to many a factory management. I could name many in Britain where the Communists, on the basis of genuine leadership offered at the shop floor level, have gained control of the shop stewards' committee and before long have come near to running the factory. More often than not, when their hold has been broken, it has not been as the result of an alternative and superior leadership being offered to the workers in the factory, but by the management being able to use some particular situation in order to get rid of the Communists by firing them. From the management's point of view, no other alternative was left to them. There has been many a strike involving thousands of non-Communist workers against the victimisation of their Communist shop stewards.

It is easy enough, in such circumstances, for pressmen to 'explain' such a situation in terms of intimidation of the rank and file by the Communist leadership, or the alleged sheep-like quality of the ordinary worker. Those in

29

industry generally know better than this. They know that, if a man is going to become a workshop leader and maintain that position, it must be on the basis of proven qualities of leadership, an ability to show results and a willingness to risk victimisation. Or, in plain English, to be so dedicated as to be prepared to lose his means of livelihood, be blacklisted by every employer in his industry and see his own standard of life and that of his loved ones go down and down as a consequence.

This, then, is the Communist approach to the question of leadership. You must believe in the human material you have at your disposal. You must not be afraid to make big demands upon it and you must skilfully and intelligently call for sacrifices, following up each such call with another.

To zeal and enthusiasm must be added understanding. In other words, the Communists recognise that if you are going to be equipped to lead in the modern world you must learn as much as possible about the things in which you believe. And you must use what you learn. But none of these things just 'happen'. The average, ordinary adult (in so far as there is such a person) is not easily enthused, does not automatically and without prompting submerge himself in a cause, sacrificing his interests to a greater one. And he does not willingly go back to school. To get all this from him, he must be inspired. And that inspiration, the Communists recognise, must come from outside. The onus is on them to create it.

For this reason, what I shall call the 'inspirational' element in the Communist approach is always very strong. This has been so from the start. Frederick Engels, Karl Marx's friend and collaborator, finished his book *Ludwig Feuerbach* with the words, 'The philosophers have only tried to explain the world; the job, however, is to change it'. That slogan of 'change the world' has proved to be one of the most dynamic of the past 120 years. Many years after Frederick Engels was dead and buried, Communist parties throughout the world made it their slogan. Some of the most sensitive men of their generation associated themselves with the Communist Party within Popular Fronts in the days of the Great Depression in the 1930s, in the belief that by so doing they were helping to 'change the world'—a world which at that moment appeared to offer nothing but unemployment, poverty, fascism and war.

Individual members of the Communist Party are brought to believe that together they and others like them can change the world. In their lifetime. They are convinced that this is not just a dream for they have techniques and a Marxist science of change-making which provide them with the means by which this can be done. When you have succeeded in making men believe that change is necessary and possible and that they are the ones who can achieve it; when you have convinced them that they and the small minority of whom they are a part can transform the world in their lifetime, you have achieved something very considerable indeed. You have put into their lives a dynamic force so powerful that you can bring them to do what would otherwise be impossible. The dull and humdrum becomes meaningful. Life becomes purposeful and immensely more worth living.

Marx concluded his Communist Manifesto with the words 'You have a world to win'. Here is a tremendous aim. In material terms, one could hardly aim higher. The belief that the world is there to be won and that Communists can win it is firmly implanted in the mind of every Communist cadre. It is with him all the time. He has a clear goal. He knows what he is working for. And it is something which he believes is capable of realisation. Moreover, a hundred times every day he is reminded that there is not only room for change but urgent need for it too. Before he has finished reading his morning paper, no matter whether it be capitalist or Communist, he has been given a dozen such reminders in reports of wars and rumours of wars, and in feature articles and analyses which provide the evidence of how far short man and his society fall of what they might be.

To the Christian there is an element of sheer tragedy in this—that people with such potentialities should give so much energy, zeal and dedication to such a cause, whilst those who believe that they have the best cause on earth often give so little to it. And their leaders are so often afraid to ask for more than the merest minimum.

The Christian may say that the Communists have the worst creed on earth. But what they have to appreciate is that the Communists shout it from the house-tops; whilst too often those who believe they have the best speak with a muted voice when they speak at all.

In a relatively short period of man's history the Communists have made an enormous impact upon its course. Our social thinking, our working conditions, our political and military programmes are different from what they might have been because this minority exists. One-third of mankind already live under their rule. The rest live differently because the Communists are there. To this limited extent they have already changed the world. But they are still far from attaining their goal, and this is a dynamic thought which drives them on.

If anyone is going to change the world for the better, it may be argued, it ought to be the Christians, not the Communists. For myself, I would say that if we started applying our Christianity to the society in which we live, then it would be we, indeed, who would change the world. Christians, too, have a world to change and a world to win. Had the early Christians gone in for slogans these might well have been theirs. They might be ours too.

There is no reason at all why they should be the monopoly of the Communists.

*   *   *   *   *

From the time that I joined the Communist Party, practically to the time when twenty years later I left it, I was conscious of the fact that our members firmly believed that, relatively few though they might be, they had a world to win and were going to win it. I came to the Catholic Church prepared for most of what I found—and it would be the sheerest hypocrisy to pretend that I either expected or found everything to be good. But one thing I had not bargained for was the many people I met who told me that the Catholic community in Britain suffered from something they described as a minority complex. I had not expected this, because I was coming from an organisation which at that time had some 45,000 members to one which was numerically 100 times as strong and which represented some 10 per cent of Britain's population.

Even in the days when we Communists could only boast some 15,000 members, we believed that when the right circumstances came, as come they must, we would make Britain Communist and would do so with the support of the mass of the people. Whatever else we may have suffered from, we had no minority complex.

Coming straight, as it were, from one world to another, it astounded me that there should be people with such numbers at their disposal, and with the truth on their side, going around weighed down by the thought that they were a small, beleaguered minority carrying on some sort of an impossible fight against a big majority. The very concept was wrong. Psychologically it was calamitous. And there was nothing in the facts, so far as I could see, to warrant such an approach.

I did not come to Catholicism expecting the calibre of

the human material to be high. We Communists had believed that the Catholic community were the most ignorant, superstitious, reactionary and obscurantist section of the British population. In practice, I found that the human material was similar to, sometimes even identical with, that which I had known within the Communist movement, which is to say that it was pretty much a cross-section of the British people. Since this was so, and remembering the use we made of our people, it seemed almost incredible that a group consisting of nearly 5 million members distributed throughout the entire community, existing in every walk of life and every stratum of society, should even begin to think in terms of a minority complex.

Most certainly the Communists do not think in such terms. Nor need they do so, so long as they continue to make it their aim that every hard-core member should be a leader. When, at the very depth of the Great Depression, when Hitler was so clearly setting out to make war and to impose his New Order upon the world, when the war clouds were gathering right round the globe, we were not depressed by the thought that our membership totalled only some 15,000. Indeed, we were almost exhilarated by the thought that the very evils of the time operated in our favour, that a situation which would be to our advantage must surely mature and that we had at our disposal 15,000 trained leaders who were operating in almost every walk of British life. We knew that we were effectively spreading our ideas far and wide. True, the course of events proved not to operate, on our sectors of the world front, as favourably as we had expected. But at that moment there was plenty of evidence to show that the ripples we created went very wide indeed into our national life each time we threw a pebble into the pool.

I am now far enough away from my Communist days

and know sufficient about the problems of the Catholic community to recognise that measuring and comparing the Communist and Catholic potentials is not just a matter of simple arithmetic. But I still do not believe, and I cannot see how anyone else can believe, that either the Catholic community or Christians generally make the maximum impact upon our thought and times of which they are capable.

If, as is so often said, the battle of our time is in the final analysis a battle for hearts and minds and souls, then this is of immense importance. Maybe, of decisive importance. In all humility we must admit that at this level the Communists have achieved far more than the Christians since the first Communist Party was formed. No useful purpose is served by Christians' pretending that the Communists' successes can all be explained in terms of trickery. Much of the Communist success has come from forms of activity and an approach to people which might as easily, and with more justification, be used by Christians.

To understand the Communist achievement one must understand the sheer mechanics, as it were, by which people, quite ordinary people with only average potentialities, can be brought to a state of mind where they are anxious to serve their cause by becoming leaders, are made into leaders and are enabled to lead effectively. As I describe the method which the Communists use, Christians and others may care to relate it to their own work.

The majority of people who join the Communist Party do so knowing very little about Communism. This is as true of the intellectuals as of the workers. The potential recruit sees the Party in action. Frequently, someone he knows is associated with it, or someone with whom he works comes to his attention because of some form of activity in which he is engaged. It may be that signatures are being collected for a peace petition, or a Communist-

led campaign is being conducted to improve working conditions or to obtain higher wages. Or he may see the Party
campaigning to prevent a widow from being evicted from
her slum dwelling. The important point is that he sees the
Party in action and he admires what it is doing. From this
he goes on to be more conscious of its other campaigns
and increasingly to feel that these correspond to real needs.
They are relevant where so much that is being done by
other bodies seems to be quite irrelevant to the titanic
needs and ills of our time.

In other words, it is the Party in action, an active,
campaigning body, and the people who make up the Party,
who normally provide the spur to the recruits' first
approach to Communism. To spell it out: recruits to Communism are usually attracted by the dedicated people who
are Communists and by the Party in action, and this action
is appealing because it appears to be concerned with real
problems. The Party operates at a level which is meaningful to the potential recruit. It comes to him, as it were; he
does not have to seek out the Party.

Pope Paul VI, when he was still Archbishop Montini
of Milan, once said that in the past it was necessary only
for the Church to ring its bell for the people to come to it.
Now, however, it is necessary for the Church to take the
bell to the people. That is something Communists long
ago learned. The irony of it is that it is they, not the
Christians, who appear to come, in the words of the song,
'with the hammer of justice, the bell of freedom and a song
about love between my brothers and my sisters all over
this land'.

The strongest impact made upon the mind of the recruit
by the first Communist with whom he associates is likely
to be of dedication. The first impression made by the
Party comes from its activity—and the apparent relevance
of that activity to our times. This being so, the man who

decides to become a Communist does so in the expectation that he, too, will have to be dedicated and active as well. This, he knows from the start, is what is involved in being a Communist. He comes to the Party, therefore, prepared to have to give of himself to an exceptional extent.

If this is the way he comes to Communism, then he knows that joining the Party is a turning-point in his life. It is quite unlike what is involved in joining any other organisation with which he is familiar. His awareness of this, particularly if he has a Christian background, is made stronger by the fact that almost inevitably he will have been making comparisons between Communists and the Communist Party on the one hand and Christians and the Church on the other. And the comparison he has made will be unfavourable to Christianity. This makes him all the more predisposed to turn to Communism and to throw himself into it, body, mind and soul.

If he has grown up in Christian circles he will know that Christianity, like Communism, demands the whole man and that Christians were intended, and are expected, to change the world. That they, too, should be active; that membership of a church is not like membership of a club. That in theory, at least, the Christian should be relating his Christianity to his whole life and to the world about him, all the time, everywhere. Yet in practice, although Christianity has taught him that total dedication is something to be admired and something to which one should aspire in one's own life, a Communist may be the first totally dedicated person he has met. Or, if that is putting it too harshly, the Communist may be the first dedicated person he has met who is not wrapped up in his own salvation but is devoting himself to the transformation of society and to changing the world.

I am not here discussing whether this impression of the Communist is justified in terms of the degree of human happiness or unhappiness which has resulted from the changes which Communism has made. I am concerned with the impact made by individual Communists and by the Party upon the man who is considering whether he should himself become a Communist. For this is a key to an understanding of why it is possible for Communists to demand so much of their members and to get it. The fact is that even as the recruit makes his decision to come into the Party he prepares himself psychologically, he predisposes himself, for big demands and a big response. If he was not prepared for this, he would not join the Party.

The process is so similar in so many cases that time after time ex-Communists have used almost identical words to describe to me the process through which they went. It goes like this: 'For years I stood on the sidelines watching the fight, admiring the Party members for all they were doing, but without being directly involved. Then some crisis in national or international affairs blew up and I came to believe that, feeling as I did, I had no right at such a time to be just a spectator when others were giving so much. I felt compelled to come in and join them in the struggle. I would have been betraying myself had I not done so.'

This image which the Party has created of totally dedicated people collectively giving all they have to their cause is such that a certain mystique has grown up quite naturally around the act of 'joining the Party'. One can think of the near-reverence in which sympathisers amongst intellectuals in the Popular Front days held those who were actually card-holding Party members. And I can recall dozens who for years had been reading Left Book Club choices and meeting for discussion who at some point or another came to me and said 'I have just got to join the Party. I have had no excuse, apart from my own desire for a quiet life and my own laziness and selfishness, for not

38

joining for a long time now. I have known that that is where I really belong. But now, in this situation, I could not live with myself if I did not join. I am ready now to make the sacrifices which will be demanded of me.'

This is not the picture which the non-Christian or the man who associates with Christians whilst not being one of them, generally has of what it means to be a Christian today. Unless or until there are Christians who are both dedicated and meaningfully active in sufficient numbers to create a similar image of Christianity, the Communists are bound to find it easier than the Christians to get the big response.

To be more specific, a man may decide to become a Catholic without its ever occurring to him that the pattern of life will be transformed, that the whole of every waking day will be different because of the set of beliefs he has accepted. It is possible for the would-be convert to go to a priest for a lengthy period of instruction without once being made to feel that he is about to become part of a group of people who are quite exceptional in their dedication. Indeed, to make him feel this might well only lead to disillusionment because it would be against truth.

It is equally possible for him to receive the whole of the instruction which is required before Baptism without hearing a word about the Church's social teaching or his personal responsibility for helping to transform society by taking Christian values—for him, probably a new scale of values—into his place of work, into his trade union or professional organisation, into his politics and into his personal relations with others. He will certainly finish his instruction knowing that he must attend Mass on Sunday, abstain from meat on Friday and say his prayers. But his instruction will in most cases end without its ever having occurred to him, because it has never been put to him and also because he has never seen it borne out in practice, that he is now one of the people who were originally charged with the job of changing the world.

In circumstances like these, the number of non-dedicated, non-active members continues to grow. Their minimal Christianity, their lack of dedication and absence of activity becomes the norm. It is a vicious circle.

The norm in the Communist Party is quite different. The consequence is that the recruits come expecting right from the start that a lot is going to be asked of them. This is tremendously important. It means that the recruit gets off on the right foot. The Party has only to underpin and maintain a concept which is already in the mind of the new member.

The new member is likely to find that this concept of the Party is justified. In Indonesia, for example, he will see top leaders of this, the largest Party of the non-Communist world, living simple lives, free of ostentation and luxury. In the United States, he will find leaders who, against a background of public hatred and contempt, spend much of their time going in and out of jail—with no possible expectation of an early change in the situation, no immediate prospect of any compensation coming in the shape of power or privilege.

I have had former Communists say to me: 'Even though I now see the evil in Communism, I still believe that when I joined the Communist Party it was the biggest and best decision I made in my life. It was the most unselfish thing I ever did.'

I understand what they mean by this. No one joining the Communist Party could suppose that life was going to be the same as before. The recruits have seen the Communists in action. They have come to know them as people and have been attracted to them because they were Communists all the time—being 100 per cent-ers in a world of 50 per cent-ers. This image of the Communists and the

Communist Party may hold back the potential recruit for some time. But if and when he makes the decision to come in, he knows that this is a turning-point. He believes that he is a better man for coming in, less than a man if he still remains outside.

The absence of any comparable Christian image—outside the religious orders—clearly creates problems for those who want to see Christians equally dedicated. The answer lies with the Christians.

CHAPTER III

The Follow Through

So the Communist recruit comes to the Party expecting to have to sacrifice and expecting also to have to go into action. He is conditioned right from the start for this. The process which follows his recruitment is therefore in the nature of a follow-up or underpinning operation. The step by step process is worth studying in some detail, not only so that we may understand how the Communists work but more especially in order to see what we have to learn from them. Where Communist organisation and training techniques are at their best the results are impressive. Any Communist who is engaged in training others knows from experience that none of the steps in the operation can be skipped and that they follow a certain order—if you like, a certain logical sequence.

The instruction of the new Party member does not normally begin immediately after he joins. Quite deliberately, and with good reason, the Party sends its new members, whenever possible, into some form of public activity before instruction begins. More specifically, it is designed to commit the recruit publicly to Communism.

Quite often this will take the form of being sent out to stand at the side of the street or in some public place selling Communist papers, periodicals or pamphlets. This may appear to be a very simple, somewhat low-grade form of activity. It is in fact of profound psychological significance. For the new recruit, still having to adjust his mind to the thought that he is now a Communist (and he knows that for large sections of the public the very name is a dirty word), this is something very significant indeed. He is making a public witness for the cause which he is now making his own. And he is, incidentally, committing himself to the Communist cause in more ways than one.

When I was a Communist I sold the Party's papers at the roadside. I hated it. Only someone who has done the same will understand what I mean. You take up your stand in some particularly public place, armed with your pile of papers. With the eyes of the world upon you, you unwrap them, feeling very self-conscious as you do so. You are convinced that everyone is wondering what you are going to produce from that parcel. You hold up a copy of the paper and you try to shout its name, and hardly recognise your own voice as you do so. The significance of all this is that, humble as the task may appear, to engage in it requires for many people a certain degree of moral courage.

As the new recruit embarks on this, his first job for the Party, he may feel such a fool that he is almost resentful at having been sent on such work. But before long he begins to see the significance of it all. For a while an unheeding public passes by, ignoring him and the paper he is trying to sell. Or, alternatively, he sees people looking at him with suspicion or even hatred. Then, perhaps, someone breaks from the passing crowd and starts abusing him. It is pretty low-level abuse. There is not much that is rational about it. The man may be a fanatical fascist, a crank, a bigot, maybe he is one of those people who believe that every evil in this world can be attributed to Communists, Jews and Freemasons. The recruit, self-consciously holding his pile of papers is embarrassed at the prospect of becoming the centre of a 'scene'. But the crowd that begins to gather is a mixed one. He now finds himself having to deal with more rational objections to his Communism. This makes him draw deeply upon such small resources as he has got in the way of knowledge of current events, of the past, present and future of Communism, of the Party's policies, philosophy, the activities of its leaders. His inclination is to take to his heels and bolt. It requires another act of moral courage to remain in a fight for which, he by now realises, he is not fully equipped. And moral courage is not a bad starting-point for future action.

The questions continue. 'Why did you join the Communist Party?' 'You don't look a bad sort of fellow, so how can you possibly join such a party when you know what Russia did in Hungary?' 'Why did Joe Stalin conclude a pact with Hitler?' 'If you're a Communist, you must be an atheist. How can anyone but a fool be an atheist today?' And so it goes on.

He gives such answers as he can. When it is all over, he heaves a sigh of relief, leaves his pitch and takes away his bundle of unsold papers. But he also takes away the knowledge that he has not got all the answers to the questions he is likely to be asked as a Communist. He is conscious now that he knows less than he thought he did. Quite probably he is dissatisfied with himself. He would dearly have loved to put up a tremendous fight for his new-found faith, taking on and defeating, or converting, all comers. He has done nothing of the sort. But he has learned his own inadequacy. This, one might say, is the beginning of wisdom.

Those who sent him into this form of activity did not expect him to have all the answers. He has let down neither the Party nor himself. In the process he has learned a good deal. When he next takes up his stand at the side of the road, he will come determined to do better. Most probably, he has been reading Communist papers in a different way, looking for the answers to the questions he was asked last time. Gathering shot and shell in readiness for the next fight. This is when he really begins to learn—and the desire to learn now comes from within himself. He is seeking to make himself more adequate, more worthy of the Party, better able to serve the cause. And his new-found thirst for knowledge about Communism, the sense of urgency which he feels as he reads and tries to understand the Communist books and papers has grown from action. Theory and action—those apparent opposites—have found a unity in his mind and in his experience.

CHAPTER IV

Study Groups at Work

FOR a while our recruit continues to be engaged in such simple forms of activity. Ones designed to commit him to a position. To give him a sense of involvement. Personal involvement in the cause. Involvement in a fight. He has made his witness for his new beliefs and because of this he now believes them more deeply, is prepared to defend them more aggressively.

Then, one day, someone who is described as the Party branch education secretary comes to him and says: 'Don't you think you ought to learn more about the Communism which you have accepted? Wouldn't you like to attend some classes? We are organising some especially for beginners. They won't make any very great demands upon you. They will be pretty simple, geared to the stage which you have now reached. We would like you to attend and we are sure that you will find them useful. If they do what we hope they will, they should fill in some of the gaps for you and help you to see the purpose of what we are all trying to do.'

He heaves a sigh of relief and thanks whatever gods there be for this timely chance of getting answers to the questions which are still worrying him. Here is a possibility of getting the shot and shell for the battle in which he is involved and the need for which he has already felt.

It is important to grasp this if we are to understand the success of the average Marxist education class. For these are normally successful in two senses. First, contrary to the experience of most other organisations, the Communists' classes quite normally hold the majority of those who enrol in them. The experience more often elsewhere is of an ever-dwindling attendance—a class begins with twenty, is down to ten half way through the series and is lucky if it finishes with seven or eight who have seen it through from start to finish. Secondly, the Communist class succeeds in the sense that the tutor gains acceptance for ideas which are in themselves fundamentally unacceptable to most people, on a subject which is, on the face of it, not immediately interesting. Perhaps the success of Communist classes of the type I have in mind is best conveyed if I state what is an indisputable fact: Communist classes change lives.

The starting point, as we have observed, is that the man who goes to them already feels a need for what the tutor has to offer. The classes meet a felt need.

This in turn means that the recruit goes to the classes in a receptive frame of mind. He does not go just out of academic interest, some vague desire to 'educate' himself. Still less does he go to argue. He goes to learn.

The tutor has something to offer which the recruit knows he needs. Something he is anxious to obtain. Therefore he is going to pay attention to what he is given. And he goes with the intention of doing whatever study is required and of putting what he learns to work in due course.

Those simple jobs which he was first given to do, such as selling papers at the side of the street or pamphlets from door to door, which cost him so much when he started, have been a psychological preparation for what now follows. It will be seen that sending new members out to make a public witness for the cause plays a tremendously important part in the subsequent success of the classes which they will attend. The process is important in the preparation of Communists as future leaders, in ensuring that they shall be active, not passive members, and in holding them to the cause.

Too often our failure to commit our own young people to our own cause leads to their subsequent defection. We fear that we shall risk too much if we make demands upon them, and we lose all as a consequence.

I recall how on one occasion I was travelling in Central Africa. An Irish Jesuit had been driving me through the bush. Then we came to the outskirts of a town. I saw that there were Africans spaced out about every 100 yards or so on either side of the road, selling a publication of some sort. As we got closer I noticed that it was *Watch Tower*. They were Jehovah's Witnesses—who, incidentally, are spreading more rapidly than Catholics in some parts of Africa today.

Since people are not normally born into the Jehovah's Witnesses I asked my companion what they had been before they joined the sect. 'A very high proportion of them,' he replied, 'were once our people. They were baptised Catholics but are now Jehovah's Witnesses.'

'When they were ours, did we give them anything to do?' I asked. 'Did we ever send them out to line the road selling papers?'

'I am afraid we didn't,' he replied. 'That is probably one reason why they are there now.'

The people concerned were quite obviously not selling very many copies of *Watch Tower*. I doubt if anyone expected that they would. The important thing was that they were making a public witness for their new-found faith. Put at its very lowest, they were being made to feel that they were doing something for a cause, whereas previously they had never been asked to go out and do anything, never made to feel any real sense of involvement.

I am not suggesting that every convert has to be sent out straight away to sell religious papers—although he could do worse, particularly if those papers have some relevance to the needs of our time and to the interests of the people who are being asked to buy them. But I believe that the Communists have proved, as others have done too, that to commit people publicly, to make them at the time of their first early enthusiasm do something which involves some degree of moral courage, which brings them before others in their new role, and submits them to the possibility of attack, can be of profound significance.

This, then, is the state of mind of the man who sets off to attend his Communist Party beginners' classes. Here he learns elementary Marxism-Leninism. He begins right at the very beginning. It is assumed that he has practically no knowledge of the subject he is discussing. He is being admitted to an unfamiliar and exciting world of thought and encouraged to learn more about a set of beliefs which challenge all other beliefs, give new interpretations, shed new light, offer explanations where others have none, lead on to a course of action which can change the world.

He will be made to feel right from the start of the very first session that instruction is not an end in itself; that acquiring knowledge may be interesting but that this should have some purpose. He is made to understand that the knowledge he gains will be so much ammunition for the fight, something to be used, not just absorbed. And he can see that this is not just words for all around him are people who are living the Communism he is being taught.

The way in which the subject matter is presented emphasises the difference between these classes and orthodox 'adult education'. If he has ever attended other adult

49

classes he will know that it is normal for quite a high proportion of the people who attend them to be there simply 'out of interest', and that others are learning simply for the sake of learning. They are the sort of people who talk a lot and do little. Armchair philosophers and bar-parlour know-alls. It would be untrue to say that there are no people at Communist classes who enjoy the sound of their own voices. But the recruit will soon see that these are the ones for whom the tutor shows the least patience or that the attention he gives them is aimed at persuading them, or pressurising them, into linking words with action.

Important too is the fact that the tutor is not simply asking his pupils to go into battle, he is quite obviously involved in it himself. The examples he uses, the anecdotes he tells, are not taken from books. They come direct from his own experience, from his contact with people and from the workaday world. The demand for total commitment implicit in the tutor's words is made acceptable by the knowledge that the tutor is himself totally committed. If he is so obviously dedicated he has the right to present the world in terms which emphasise the need for dedication.

Inspirational Approach

When Communist tutors are being trained (I trained them myself at one time in London) they are taught that the way in which they present their subject matter is of immense importance. And the method of presentation normally follows the same pattern.

Communists prove in practice that it does not matter how dull a subject may be, it can still be presented in an inspiring way. It is up to the tutor to discover how this can be done. This calls for thought and for ingenuity. But above all else, he must himself be inspired.

In his work, the tutor has the help of the Party's Education Department who prepare the syllabus which he will use. Consider, for example, the one which our recruit will take when he attends his first classes. It is called 'A Course for New Members'. There are four lessons in elementary, scientific socialism, a mixture of Marxian economics and philosophy. To many people economics and philosophy sound like the dullest of subjects. The average Communist recruit has very little knowledge of either but anything he knows predisposes him to believe that they are intrinsically dull. What the tutor has to teach is not simple, although it is made as simple as possible. How then to make it inspirational, how engage and hold the attention of a group of people who not long ago would have groaned at the very thought of the subjects to which they are now being introduced?

The titles given to the four lessons, enumerated on the cover of the syllabus provide a key to the answer. They are:

(1) The kind of world we live in.
(2) How that world can be changed.
(3) The force that can change it.
(4) The Communist Party, the party of the working class.

Here is economics and philosophy plus. 'The philosophers have only tried to explain the world, the job however is to change it. . . .' Engels's words take on flesh. Philosophy and economics in this beginners' class are used for a purpose. It is a grand, heroic, challenging one, no less than the changing of the world.

Again, it is not a question of the tutor's simply saying so. The subject matter is presented in such a way as to relate the life and experience of those before him to the task of changing the world. Very quickly the recruit is made to feel that the Communist Party is going to change it. It is for this that the Party exists. By becoming a member he has become one of those who are already doing it. Now, by attending these classes, he too is learning how to do it and to do it effectively and rapidly. He is qualifying to be right in the front rank of those everywhere who are engaged in this great operation.

The course is very basic, everything he learns is presented as simply as the subject permits. Nonetheless, it takes him to the very roots of Marxism. Implicit in the wording of the syllabus, in the approach of his tutor, in the very way in which he was first invited to attend the classes is the thought that this is a serious undertaking by seriously-minded, adult people. Even as the recruit is being instructed, he is also being inspired. The instruction is all the more acceptable to him because it is inspirational. Any well-trained Communist tutor will, then, believe that the starting-point must be the inspirational approach.

Global Struggle

Next, the subject matter is presented in global terms. It is presented against the background of a world in conflict. The recruit is made to feel that there is a great battle going on all over the world. That this includes his own country, his own town, his own neighbourhood, the block of flats in which he lives, the factory or office where he works.

He is made to feel also that the period of history in which he happens to be living is a decisive one and that he personally has a decisive role to play. He is part of a great, worldwide movement which is challenged on all sides, confronted by an implacable enemy and involved in a battle which will decide the course of history for generations ahead.

The words the tutor uses, and those the recruit reads in

his little syllabus, appear purely 'educational'. Yet, in the impact they make on his mind, they are akin to war propaganda. They are designed to make him, metaphorically, ready to demand that a gun should be put in his hand, that he should be given ammunition and sent straight into the fight. Indeed, in a very real sense this is what happens. Certainly, the Communist Party itself sees Marxism as a weapon to be used and makes its followers see it and use it in this way.

The battle, he is taught, is worldwide. It is global. On the one side is suffering, toiling, sweating humanity. All the underdogs, all the underprivileged of this world. Those who suffer poverty, those who live under colonialism. Those who die from preventable social diseases and those who die from wars which are the inevitable, foreseeable and preventable product of the evil capitalist system.

Vaguely, in the past our recruit has felt himself to be on the side of those who suffer. He has numbered himself amongst the reformers, those who want change. But this is change with a difference. It is fundamental, root-and-branch change. And the sense of oneness which he has with those for whom his new cause claims to speak is soon made greater by the way in which the subject matter is presented at the classes he is attending.

Here is another key to an understanding, one of many, to the dynamism of the world Communist movement.

I suppose it is true to say that most converts from one cause to another must inevitably feel a certain sense of deprivation. I have frequently discussed this with Anglican clergymen who have become Catholics. There was a world of meaning, and an immense sense of loss, behind the words of one who told me: 'For years as I stood at my altar I believed that I held God in my hands. Then one day I came to believe that I did not. I ceased to be a priest and now am a schoolteacher. I had no alternative, if I

53

was going to pay any regard to my integrity at all but to become a Catholic. But my sense of deprivation is very real indeed, despite all that I have gained.'

And I recall the wistfulness of another who talked to me of the tremendous sense of ministry he had felt when he was a Protestant clergyman and how this, inevitably, had gone when he became a Catholic layman.

My own sense of deprivation when I came from Communism to Catholicism took a different form. It was the loss of that sense of oneness which we had in the Communist Party. Catholics talk about membership of the Mystical Body of Christ. But very few *feel* that sense of oneness which the Communist feels with men everywhere. Of course, the Communist's sense of oneness, if it is not a contradiction in terms, is a selective oneness. There are those he loves and those he hates. The overwhelming majority are his potential allies, the ones with whom he identifies himself. The other, a minority, are their exploiters. Hard-faced employers, rapacious landlords, scheming imperialists. He may not necessarily hate them as individuals, but he is certainly taught to hate them collectively. And that hatred goes all the deeper because he sees them as the small group who stand between men and the ending of injustices, who block the road to progress, by their actions and their policies perpetuate a system which can bring only suffering to mankind and which impedes the development of that other system by means of which man will for the first time truly come into his own.

But no matter how much one has to qualify the 'oneness' created by the global terms in which the beginner's Communism is taught to him, it is real enough. It is immensely important in his life.

The thought of world unity has a particular appeal today. No earlier generation ever had the means by which men throughout the world might be truly and actively united. It is only now that world unity becomes possible, as access to every part of the world is made available to increasing numbers of people, as transport is speeded up and nation can talk to nation by means of radio and television. This desire for world unity expressed itself in practical form in the creation of the League of Nations. When the League failed, with the coming of World War II, the idea of world unity was not jettisoned. On the contrary, the second world war gave birth to the United Nations. But the unity the Communist is offered appears to go deeper, for it is based upon an already existent worldwide movement, a commonly shared philosophy, a commonly accepted goal.

The deep division which has developed in the world Communist movement inevitably weakens this image, which is one of the many reasons why Communists themselves must feel that it is urgently necessary that the breach should be healed. Yet it still remains true that one of the most powerful forces in the life of the individual Communist is a sense of oneness first, with the underprivileged and exploited everywhere and secondly, with people who share his own aims and outlook, his own form of organisation and discipline and who together constitute that élite which will in due course make an end of all underprivilege and exploitation. This grows out of, and is fed by, constant insistence by the Communist leaders and theoreticians that their movement is a global movement involved in a global struggle.

Instruction for Action

Next, the instruction the recruit receives is from the start linked with action. It is made meaningful to those who receive it. It is the tutor's job to somehow connect it up with real life in every way. Each person being instructed must be made to feel that, no matter how theoretical the subject, what he is being taught is meaningful to him in his life and meaningful to the world and times in which he lives. The tutor sees his job as not simply that of pumping so much information into the heads of so many people but rather that of giving them instruction which will lead almost automatically on to action.

Any Communist tutor who is worth his salt finishes each class with these words: 'What are the comrades going to do about what they have learned today? How are *you* going to apply it to the hospital where you are nursing? *You* in the school where you teach? *You* in the factory where you are employed? *You* as a housewife to the neighbourhood where you are living?'

The first item on the agenda when the class next meets will be: 'How did the comrades apply what they learned last week?' It does not matter whether the subject is trade union history, scientific socialism or dialectical materialism, teacher and taught must try to relate it to life and action.

In passing, I would reiterate that this is not the way in which Christianity, for example, is normally taught. The man who is under instruction to become a Catholic may—or may not, as the case may be—be taught a certain amount of basic doctrine. If the priest who is instructing him is particularly good, he may finish his instruction knowing the fundamentals of his faith fairly well. But in the normal 'converts class' rarely if ever is any attempt made to link what is taught with action, except in terms of absolutely minimal 'duties'. It is stretching things very far indeed to suggest that this is relating religion to action and to life.

It is highly unlikely that the points of doctrine which the convert is taught will at every turn be related to action

56

and that, step by step, he will be brought to see that his thought and behaviour, not only on Sunday morning, on Friday and at some point during Lent, but all the time, must now be different from what it was. That what he is being taught must profoundly influence his behaviour on the Stock Exchange, in the employers' organisation, in the factory and trade union, wherever his normal life takes him. In the circumstances, since so little is asked of Christians by their leaders, and so much is asked of Communists by theirs, Christians have small cause for complaint if they seem to make little impact upon the larger community of which they are part, whilst a handful of Communists succeed in making people aware of their presence the whole of the time.

The Fight Against Evil

Communist teachings are presented in such a way as to make the individual attending 'Party education classes' feel that he is engaged in a fight against evil things and on behalf of what is good. You may well say that this is an extraordinary inversion of the true situation. But you must not expect the Communists to believe that.

The Communist feels deeply that the capitalist society under which we live, and the remnants of feudalism which still persist in important parts of the world, are evil. Not unnaturally, therefore, he sees those who in any way are engaged in perpetuating the present system as evil too. Evil in their beliefs, evil in their actions.

To him our system of society is inherently unjust, and inhuman. There was a time when, despite this, it was 'progressive'. It led men on from a lower state to a higher one. It released great productive forces, opened the way for man's ingenuity and inventiveness, so making possible a higher standard of life than had ever before been known.

But social systems come and go. They are 'progressive' in their early days, they reach a point where they have made their real contribution to the evolution of man, then go into decline. And a decadent society brings little but suffering on an ever-increasing scale to those who live in it. Two appalling world wars in which human life and human suffering became quite meaningless have been just one of the products of capitalism in its final 'imperialist' phase.

From the Communist point of view, the real evil lies in the fact that, since capitalism is an acquisitive society, based upon the profit motive, individual capitalists, and the ruling class and their hangers-on collectively, actually profit by the slaughter of war, by the suffering of the people of the underprivileged areas of the world. This thought that there are people who have a vested interest in human suffering can be a tremendous spur to action in the life of the Communist.

All this helps to make him feel that he is engaged in a great crusade against something which is unspeakably evil. In his heart, as he works in no matter how small a way for the Communist cause, he feels a deep loathing for the social system against which he is working, a profound hatred for those who seek to perpetuate it.

This is part of the psychology of war. If you are going to win a war you must make your people believe that they are fighting against monstrously evil things. That individually and collectively the enemy either deserves to be fought or must in any case be fought so that an evil system may be destroyed. You must make your people feel that their side represents what is good. Willingness to give all to the cause of victory will most easily be engendered if, particularly in the early stages, you can make your people believe that they are fighting on behalf of someone, some group, some nation which is the actual or potentially helpless

STUDY GROUPS AT WORK

victim of a powerful foe. It may be 'gallant little Belgium', it may be their own wives who will be raped and their children killed should the enemy succeed.

The Communists achieve this sense of crusading, not simply by an overheated 'war' propaganda amongst their own members (although they do not hesitate to use this among the general public). They achieve it at a deeper level, by 'Marxist education', and by the method, the means, by which it is taught. The little child dying of starvation on the sidewalks of Calcutta can be as great a spur to the Communist to go out and sacrifice his time, energy, money, if necessary life, as was 'little Belgium' to any British Tommy who responded to the call for volunteers in 1914.

Quite apart from this 'war propaganda' aspect of the subject, the point we are considering is that Communist instruction is presented in such a way that the Party member is convinced that he is on the side of good, and involved in a struggle against evil. This appeals to something deep in his nature, something good. In their hearts, many men, perhaps most men, like to feel that they are on the side of righteousness. The Communist is brought to believe precisely this. What was, when he first joined, little more than a vague 'feeling' that he was identifying himself with a cause which is on the side of good, is transformed into a deep intellectual conviction.

An immense amount flows from this. One reason why the Communist is prepared to make his exceptional sacrifices is that he believes he is taking part in a crusade, he is on the side of righteousness. His total dedication is really no more mysterious than the fact that millions of men could, almost knowingly, march straight into a mincing machine to be chewed to bits in senseless battles between 1914 and 1918. They left home and loved ones, prospects and careers, almost anxious to throw away their young lives. Dedication of this type is normal in time of war. By creating a similar psychology, the Communists in time of peace get the response that goes with it.

To the Christian it may seem extraordinary that an atheist tutor can convince a group of others whom he is instructing in an atheist creed that they are part of a great crusade fighting on the side of good. In fact, this would appear simply to prove man's deep need for a cause, for a faith. It is evidence of modern man's spiritual hunger.

Communist propagandists know that Communism has both an economic and an ethical appeal. To one man, it will be the economic appeal which will be most powerful. He is most likely to be the one who is at the receiving end of poverty, underpayment or unemployment. To another the ethical appeal will be the greater. This will most probably be the deeper and more enduring of the two. In practice, the Communists usually combine the ethical with the economic, even when they are appealing to the man at the 'receiving end'.

Anyone who has ever led a strike which is being fought on a 'bread and butter issue' knows perfectly well that if it is going badly and the morale of the strikers threatens to decline and crack, then, if you really want to give it a boost, you must stop talking economics and switch to the ethical appeal. You get away from simply stressing that the strike is for so many extra pence an hour and insist that there is a tremendous principle at stake. That way you maintain morale and increase the willingness to fight to a finish.

The Communists use this. Basically, they appeal to something that is good.

They appeal to people's capacity for moral indignation. Moral indignation can, and often does, look like cant. It can be hypocritical. The Communists have helped to make it so, because theirs is a selective moral indignation. Yet,

60

in itself, the appeal to moral indignation is not necessarily an unhealthy thing. Editorial leader writers can treat it as though it is something which merits only sneers. Catholics, I have observed, tend in particular to view it with suspicion. One fears that often those who write and think in these terms are themselves so cynical that they have become incapable of feeling moral indignation, which suggests that they are spoiled idealists. If so, they are that much poorer for it, that much less men.

Certainly, the Communists create and use moral indignation for their own purposes and do so very effectively indeed. By the time the recruit to Communism has done his first lesson on 'The world in which we live' and the second on 'How to change it' he, at any rate, will feel this moral indignation as a powerful force in his life—as it is intended that he should. The printed syllabus, when he first looked inside it, threatened some dull classes ahead. Instead, he finds them exciting, stimulating, relevant to everything that means anything in his new life. This is, to summarise, achieved by the presentation of the subject matter in terms which are heroic, global, relevant, linked to action and by the tutor's ability to make him believe that he is now involved on the right side in the age-old fight between good and evil, and that the movement to which he belongs has the means to ensure the ultimate victory. The change in his thinking and his behaviour is profound.

CHAPTER V

The Story of Jim

EARLY in the last war I was conducting a leadership training course for a group of Communists in a London borough. I ended my last lecture in this series by saying that the Communist Party could take anyone who was willing to be trained in leadership and turn him into a leader. I stepped down from the rostrum and there, awaiting me, was Jim.

A relatively new member of the Party, he was almost pathetically anxious to be turned into a leader. He took me up on the words with which I had concluded the lecture. And as I looked at him I thought that I had never seen anyone who looked less like a leader in my life. He was just about the most unprepossessing man I had ever seen.

He was very short, grotesquely fat, with a flabby white face, a cast in one eye and, to make matters worse, a most distressing stutter.

I am not making fun of him—it is very germane to my story—when I say that quite literally he came to me and said: 'C-c-c-comrade, I w-w-w-want you to t-t-t-take me and t-t-t-turn me into a l-l-leader of m-m-m-men.' I looked at Jim and I wondered how I was going to do it. Then I thought to myself: 'Well I told the class that we could take anyone who was willing to be trained in leadership and turn him into a leader, and here is Jim pathetically anxious for me to do it. This is a challenge.' So I set about the job.

It will be observed that I had made only one qualification. This was that the would-be leader must be willing to be trained. This presupposes a certain attitude of mind, which Jim already had. It was, so far as I could see at that moment, almost the only thing I had to build on.

The experience of the Communists is that if you are going to turn a man into a leader you must first give him confidence in himself. Jim, like so many others but with more reason, had no confidence in himself and appeared to have no basis for it in any case.

The second thing is that you must give him something to be confident about. This world is full of people possessed of an overdose of self-confidence but with nothing to back it up. Despite what they may think about the matter, these are not leaders. One look at Jim was enough to tell me that he had practically nothing to be confident about. So he had to be given some basis for self-confidence.

I told him: 'If you attend the classes which the Party branch organises and learn the things we can teach you there, we will give you the answers to all the great questions which trouble the mind of modern man. We will explain the universe to you, so that you will come to see that, since they are dialectical, the very laws of the universe operate on the side of the ultimate victory of Communism. What we teach you will enable you to see the world through new eyes, recognising the forces that make for change.

'We will give you a new approach to history, explaining the story of man in such a way that you will come to understand what the common people have been suffering and what they have been able to achieve throughout the ages. We will show you that there is a pattern in history; that the whole history of man has been building up towards the coming revolution and the victory of Communism. This is the very essence of the historical and dialectical materialism which, in due course, we shall teach you too.

'When you learn this, you will discover that all progress comes from conflict. This means that when you and the Party engage in strikes and tenants' movements, when you participate in the class war, you are identifying yourself with this law by means of which change is brought about. You will not only work for change, you will understand the inner nature of change and man's ability to identify himself with those laws of the physical universe and of history by means of which change occurs.

'This means that you will not be acting blindly. You will make yourself the conscious and willing instrument of an historic process. And you will know that there are others like you, millions of us all over the world doing the same.

'When the moment of opportunity comes here in Britain you will be one of this minority, one of the few, who because of their understanding of these things, will be able to overturn this rotten old society in which we live, guide the people through the revolution and on to the building of a Britain which belongs to the common people and is part of a grand new world.'

As a consequence of that first pep-talk, I set him on the road to achieving a new self-confidence. I gave him something to believe in, helped him to believe in himself. He undoubtedly had an inferiority complex when he came to me. It was not long, I imagine, before we had given him a messianic complex instead.

What I had told him was reinforced at the classes which he attended. He now believed in something, he had a goal and saw that he would have a role in its achievement. Before long you could watch his personality unfold.

After he had undergone some months of instruction I had another heart-to-heart talk with him. I told him that he was now ready to be a tutor and should prepare to go into this new form of work. He was terrified. 'W-w-w-what m-m-m-me!' he exclaimed. I replied by reminding him that when he first joined the Communist Party he, like so many others who had come to it, knew practically nothing about Communism as such. He had come into it through one of its campaigns. I asked him whether he had learned very much in the past few months. He replied that he had.

'But the people who are just coming into the Party as recruits know as little about Communism as you did when you first came in,' I told him. 'This means that on the basis of what you have learned you now know much more than they do. The whole art of teaching is to know just a little bit more than the people you are trying to teach. If you have this, then you can get away with it. Moreover, if they ask you questions to which you do not have the answers, you must admit this, tell them that you will give them the answers next time you meet, then go to your textbooks and find them. That way you will learn.'

By this means I made him believe that he could do it. I persuaded him that he, an ordinary worker, very new to the Communist Party and with more than his fair share of physical and psychological difficulties, had something that others hadn't got and he therefore also had a duty to try and pass it on.

Throwing him into tutorial work in this way was an essential part of his training as a leader. He had at once to begin to think in new terms. For months ideas had been pumped into his head. Now he had to get some order into his thinking. He must learn to formulate those ideas, then pass them on to other people in simple language which they could understand; first to a small group and then later, I hoped, to larger ones.

He was an electrician, a building worker employed on a building site along with many other workers. I did not send him off to teach dialectical materialism to nuclear physicists. Much more significantly, I sent him to teach a beginners' course and the people he taught were ordinary building workers like himself, drawn from the same building site. By day they were so many building workers, together sharing the work and the mud and the inconveniences of life on a great building job. But at night he became the teacher with his own workmates sitting at his feet as his pupils. The whole relationship was changed. He had something which they had not. It was something they wanted. And it was to him, the man who, on the face of it, appeared to have so much less than they, that they had to turn. This, of course, immensely increased his confidence in himself and his self-respect. His personality grew still further.

If he was to succeed with them, he had to understand sufficiently well what he had learned to be able to put it in their language. He had to get the ideas out of his head into theirs. He had to become articulate. I am sure that when he began he was terrified. But before long, talking to a very small group of people who knew less than he about the subject under discussion, he found himself earnestly explaining it to them and becoming articulate in the process.

It is worth noting that, before we put him on to his tutorial work, we gave him a thorough training in it, teaching him both the subject and the method of tuition simultaneously. So he was sent into the fight prepared for it in advance. And, of great psychological importance, he knew that whilst we had encouraged him to go into it, we had also taken the trouble to equip him for it.

I left him to his tutorial work for some time. The reports which came to me indicated that after a nervous start he was now making good progress and those who passed through his hands genuinely learned from him what we wanted them to know. Thus, simultaneously, we were training a tutor, teaching beginners and developing a leader.

Then, one day, I went to him again and this time suggested that he should do a public speaking course with a view to engaging in the Party's agitation and public propaganda. Again, he was appalled at the thought. But he knew, nonetheless, on the basis of his experience of tutorial work that he had unsuspected potentialities. So he went. We did not turn him into a great orator, we did not even entirely cure him of his stutter, although, as he gained confidence in himself this became modified and finished up as a noticeable but not entirely unhelpful impediment in his speech. It was often the case, when we put him up in the market place to address a public meeting, that he would get the sympathy of a crowd and hold it more easily than others who had not his disabilities. It seemed as though an ordinary fair-minded British crowd felt that if this man who had so many excuses for not getting up on the platform and facing a hostile audience was nonetheless prepared to do so, then at least he deserved a hearing.

Once he had established himself as an effective propagandist and agitator, able to exert his influence over a crowd, I took him on to the next stage of his training. I told him that he ought never to drop either his tutorial or his street-corner work. But his real field of leadership lay elsewhere. So far his training had been in the direction of leadership in general. Now he must provide leadership in a particular sphere of activity, the one where he could be most effective and which was most naturally his. There was no doubt about the choice: it should be within his own industry, on the job and in the trade union. Particularly the trade union.

It is a rule of the Communist Party that each Party member must be a member also of his appropriate trade union. Jim was already, therefore, an organised trade unionist. But hitherto he had been an inactive one. Now, I told him, he must become active. He must take the qualities of leadership, which we had brought to the surface, into his local trade union branch. But just as we had prepared him for his tutorial work, then for his street-corner agitation, so now we prepared him for his new form of activity. We did not throw him to the wolves, or, to change the metaphor, we did not send him into battle untrained, unprepared.

For months he attended classes by way of preparation —trade union history, trade union procedure, the history of the broader labour movement and of the working class. There, too, he learned the very vocabulary of the trade union movement.

A group of hard-headed trade unionists soon suspects a man who appears suddenly on the scene, dominating the discussion with the quite obvious intention of grinding his own particular axe or riding his own personal hobby horse. It is here, incidentally, that Catholics who in recent years have gone into the trade union movement have most frequently gone wrong. The man who simply forces his own beliefs down the throats of his hearers, using, in this case, the vocabulary of the Catholic social doctrine class, not of the trade union branch, remains an outsider. If he only makes a contribution to discussion when some allegedly 'Catholic' subject can be forced before those present, such as opposition to the proposed opening of a

68

birth control clinic, or, as at election time, the need for a square deal for Catholic schools, is heard with little sympathy—and deservedly so.

There are plenty of self-educated men in the labour movement who know their trade union history as part of their lives; the great industrial struggles of the past, out of which present legislation and present attitudes grew, are deep in their consciousness. But the man who can get up and refer casually and convincingly to the Taff Vale Judgment of 1901, or the 'Trades Dispute Act of 1927', or talk of 'the Triple Alliance' and 'Black Friday' is instinctively assumed not only to know what he is talking about but also to be someone to whom trade unionism is truly meaningful in its own right.

It was this that we gave Jim. It was not long before he had one of the top positions in his local branch. Then, he was elected to the area committee of his union and was also made a Federation shop steward on the building site.

In time he became a national leader within his own industry. When he died a few years ago, his death was of sufficient importance to warrant a front-page report in the *Daily Worker* and many of his fellow-workers and trade unionists followed his body to the crematorium. Jim, the most unpromising-looking piece of human material that ever came my way had become a leader of men.

*   *   *   *   *

Jim's story says much of what can be said about the training of a leader as the Communists see it. First, I inspired him, gave him the clearly-defined goal of a new and better world and the belief that he and others could between them achieve it provided that they prepared themselves sufficiently for the moment of opportunity. I gave him a sense of involvement in a battle, and the conviction that by going to classes he would gain the arms and ammunition required for the fight.

The classes he attended were geared to his needs. What he learned was presented in terms which were understandable to him as a worker. The classes he attended were small ones. We shall come to this later, but this is of great significance. There, he was an individual and in the intimacy of the small group could, despite his reticence, be brought to make his contribution to discussion.

By making him a tutor, we gave him confidence in himself, enabled him to glimpse his own unsuspected potentialities. By making him a tutor, too, we made him think in an organised way, sifting what was relevant from that which was irrelevant; he learned, because he had to, how to get the ideas out of his head into the heads of others. He was made articulate. We gave him knowledge which others had not got and an intelligently selected group to whom this could be passed on. By training him, then putting him up to speak in the market-place and at the street corner we showed him that he could influence larger bodies of people, too. We helped him to grow in stature when we thus brought him before the public eye as one of the Party's leading local figures. Then we gave him specialised training in preparation for the sphere of activity in which he could be most effective, where there was the biggest job to be done, and which lay nearest to hand.

This, I believe, is a pattern which others might follow.

Communism in practice is shot through with paradoxes. Here in the case of Jim, as in the case of so many others, there is indeed a great paradox. The opponents of Communism say that Communism is the great enemy of the individual man. That Communists think in terms of the masses, not of individuals. That human freedom and human personality are crushed by Communism. Philosophically all this is true. This is true, also, of its practice, as demonstrated in the countries where it rules.

Yet, on the other hand, it is also conspicuously true that the individual member of the Communist Party who undergoes its training and its formation frequently blossoms as a personality. People who have been seen as failures by other organisations are frequently turned by the Communists into successes. Men who have been by-passed or rejected by others, who seem too ordinary, too mediocre to be even considered as leaders, are shown by the Communists to have potentialities of leadership, nonetheless.

I can think of many a lapsed-Catholic Communist who has told me that when he was practising the Faith the greatest responsibility he was ever given was to help, along with others, to move the chairs in the parish hall 'for Father'. Inside the Communist Party he was made to feel that he had something better than that to offer. And events proved that this was so.

I think of the old illiterate but intensely intelligent and characterful peasant woman in the Philippines who had left the Catholics to join Ecclesia Christi—a breakaway sect of recent origin. When I asked her why she had done this, she replied that when she was a Catholic no one had ever given her anything to do. Now as a member of Ecclesia Christi she was out every night organising small group meetings in the homes of the people in the barrios throughout the area where she lived.

The Communists show confidence in the Jims of this world where others ignore them. They demonstrate in practice all too frequently a greater faith than we in the human material that God puts into our hands. No Christian can draw much comfort from this thought. It must be seen as a challenge. For the leadership training process which I have described is not inherently evil, there is nothing fundamentally unethical about it. There was nothing we did to Jim which might not have been done by others on behalf of a more worthy cause.

CHAPTER VI

The Formation Process

IT is in the study group that Communist leaders are formed. There, the potentialities of the individual are discovered, drawn out and canalised.

Part of the secret of the Communists' success in what they call Marxist education, and what their opponents call indoctrination, lies in the actual methods which they employ. It goes without saying that some of the Communist instruction is achieved by means of lecture series of the conventional type, where the lecturer talks for perhaps forty-five minutes or one hour and then takes questions from the audience. This method they would normally regard as suitable only for preparing the way for more intensive study by their members or, alternatively, as a method of mass education.

When they want to get their ideas across to a group of their own members as a means of making these into cadres or of improving the quality of existing cadres, they use different methods. Through small study groups they aim (1) to teach Marxism, (2) to equip those who attend them to go into effective action for the cause; (3) in the process of teaching them, to contribute to their training as leaders.

If these aims are to be achieved, it is important that the tutor should have them firmly fixed in his mind both when he is preparing for and conducting a class. Each tutor is expected as he prepares his notes to ask himself the question, 'education for what?'

This is a question which Catholic and other educators might well regularly ask themselves as well. Too often the purpose is lost sight of and we then have a situation where priests, nuns and teaching brothers, who years earlier followed their vocation believing that this called for total dedication, get so caught up in the job of teaching that the original purpose recedes into the background and they begin to measure success only in terms of academic achievements—achievements which, incidentally, could almost certainly be those of lay teachers. This is not only a waste of priests and religious, it is a waste of opportunities too.

But the Communist tutor is expected to remind himself over and over again that he is not just concerned with passing on knowledge to people. His aim is to equip them for action and to assist them to become leaders.

The subject being taught and the existing level of understanding of those attending the classes will determine which of a number of methods the tutor should use. The three most typical are (1) lecture followed by questions, discussion or both; (2) 'controlled discussion'; (3) question and answer method.

Of the three, (2) is the one which is regarded as the most useful, where circumstances are right. It is when this method is used that the aim of developing qualities of leadership and drawing out the potentialities of those attending the classes is most likely to be realised. From the tutor's point of view this is the most difficult. These are the lines it normally follows:

Ideally, the number of people taking the course should not be less than three or four nor more than fourteen or fifteen. Since the aim will be to involve everyone in discussion, too small a number will obviously lead to too narrow an exchange of ideas. If too many are present, then the naturally silent ones will remain silent. It will be impossible to bring everyone into the discussion.

Immense attention has to be paid to detail. For example, even the way in which those present are seated is important. Ideally, they should be in a circle around the tutor in a relaxed, informal, yet serious atmosphere.

The tutor does not follow the conventional practice of delivering a lecture and then taking questions. His success may to a very great extent be measured by the extent to which he is able to get those present to do the talking and to say what he would have said had he been giving them a lecture.

By way of preparation, class members will have been given in advance a list of 'necessary reading'. It is recognised that those who go to such classes are likely to be busy people, who will be coming to learn at the end of a hard working day. They are also, in most cases, Party activists. Clearly the time available to them for reading is limited. Any reading done can only be at the expense of some other form of Communist activity.

Therefore, the necessary reading is cut to a minimum. Chapter I of the *Communist Manifesto*, perhaps eight or nine pages of *Wage, Labour and Capital*, a few pages of a recently-published pamphlet, maybe a chapter or two of a book by Lenin. The selection is made with great care by the Party headquarters' Education Department.

This serves a double purpose: The class member will be far more likely to do all that is required if not too much is asked of him, but, also, he will be conscious of the fact that someone else who prepared the syllabus has given a lot of time and thought to the job of trying to save him time. He therefore feels a link with the unnamed people in the Party Education Department who prepare the syllabi.

75

He is likely to tell himself that they understand the problems of people like him. In due course, when the classes get under way, he will quickly learn that the necessary reading really is necessary. Without it he will be unable to understand fully the line the discussion takes.

The tutor prepares himself for the discussion as though he was going to give a lecture. In other words, he prepares the logical framework of the lecture, limiting himself to perhaps three main points for which he hopes to gain acceptance. But he will set out so to lead and control the discussion as to get every member of the class talking on each major point.

He then makes the 'opening statement'. In this he briefly outlines the subject which will be discussed at this particular session, putting into rather less words the outline already contained in the printed syllabus which everyone present has already studied. This opening statement will probably last not more than four or five minutes, ten minutes at the most. Then he will break off and set about the task of trying to get everyone talking.

In such a group, almost invariably, there will be someone to whom all too obviously talking is no difficulty. Later on, he will probably have to be silenced, otherwise he will dominate the discussion, but in the opening stages he is immensely useful. The tutor turns to him and says: 'Well, comrade, what are your views on the point I have just made?' The incurable talker starts talking. It is almost immaterial whether he is saying what the tutor wants ultimately to have said, or whether he is saying its opposite. When he has talked for long enough the tutor, who has been watching the faces of the others, has probably already seen that someone else is itching to come into the discussion, either to take up one of his own points or, possibly, to controvert something said by the 'talker'. The tutor brings number two in. And so he continues,

76

switching from one to another, putting in a word here and there of his own in order to unobtrusively direct the discussion in the way he wants it to go.

Just as almost any such group contains at least one incurable talker, so it is likely also to include at least one 'silent' member. He is the sort of man who finds it difficult to talk in front of others. This does not necessarily mean that he does not think, or for that matter, that he is incapable of deep thought. In practice, the 'talker' is frequently a more facile thinker than the 'silent' member. But the tutor's aim is to get everyone talking, including the silent ones.

This is not just as an exercise in ingenuity. The purpose is to develop everyone present and this can only be done by making them articulate. And so, sooner or later, the tutor must set out deliberately to bring the silent one in. If he is anything of a psychologist at all he will know that if he shoots a direct question at such a person he will almost certainly send him further into himself and strike him dumb. He therefore quietly and casually turns to him and asks whether, since he alone has not yet expressed a point of view, he has some doubts or difficulties. If so, if he would care to put these before the group, perhaps they might be able to help him overcome them. If he in fact has no 'doubts' or 'difficulties' the matter is soon cleared up. But let us take the case of a man who has.

The tutor's approach to his silence serves a treble purpose. The member is made to feel that any doubts he has may be overcome, that the mere fact that he has them is, as it were, due to some shortcoming on his part which he will want to rectify, and that the others are all anxious to help him in this.

The rest of the group for their part, having now collectively arrived at some agreed opinion, apparently on

77

the basis of their own discussion, and of their own voli-
tion, are eager to seize this first opportunity of converting
someone else to their new-found point of view.

Everyone present, it seems, is anxious to help him with
his 'difficulties'. This is an atmosphere to which he is
likely to respond. Before long he is feeling that his failure
to go along with the others is perhaps due to some fault
in himself, some inability to see the obvious, and so he
takes a new and more critical approach to his own point
of view which, in all probability, he revises. Everyone is
delighted when together they have got him past his difficulty and the group can then move on to discussion of
the next major point.

Except in the case of someone who is clearly so hostile,
cantankerous or unco-operative that there is no possible
hope of his being persuaded, the tutor will not normally
move on to discussion of the second point he wants them
to accept, until all have collectively and individually
accepted his first.

The value of this method is that the ideas do not appear
to come from the tutor, but from the class members, who
do not feel that he is imposing his ideas upon them. And
since they, by means of their own thought and discussion
have arrived at these conclusions, they will go away convinced that these are their own opinions and beliefs,
arrived at on the basis of reading, thought and discussion.

This is politically important. Others may talk of Communist 'indoctrination'. Those who have been taught by
this method are likely angrily to reject such a description
of their instruction. They will feel even more strongly
when their opponents describe this as 'brainwashing'. Anti-
Communist propaganda which describes them as 'dupes
of Moscow' will seem to them to be quite transparently
malicious and untruthful. Over and over again in the

Communist Party it is said with the deepest conviction that 'nowhere on earth is there more discussion than in the Communist Party'. It is said with pride and in the belief that it is the ultimate and incontrovertible refutation of all such charges made by their opponents.

It is certainly the case that the average Communist comes away from a class at which the 'controlled discussion' method has been used feeling that the views which they have all accepted that evening are the sort that any reasonable group of people might be expected to adopt once their minds were cleared of prejudices and propaganda. Individually, each member feels that the point of view which has been accepted is his. He helped to think it out, he contributed to discussion and by his own efforts and those of others, arrived at it only after all preconceived and false ideas had been cleared out of the way. Henceforth it will be his and he will defend it as his own.

The second most favoured tutorial method used by the Communists is the 'Question and Answer' method, which bears a close similarity to the first.

In both cases it is necessary that those attending should have done the 'necessary reading'. Those who fail to do this before the first session are quickly put on the spot by the method used. When questions are asked by the tutor, and others present begin to come up with the right answers, he is left bewildered and far behind. Normally, no one will censure him for this but he will leave in a self-critical mood, somewhat chastened by his inability to show up well and determined that he will put in the relatively short but necessary time required for the reading which has, in any case, already been so thoughtfully reduced to a minimum by the comrades at headquarters.

No matter which method may be used, the tutor, like the taught, is given maximum help by those who direct this branch of the Party's work. The member has his

79

syllabus, the tutor has his Tutors' Guide which has been specially prepared for the syllabus he is taking.

The Party explains the 'Question and Answer' method in one such 'Guide' as follows:

'The classes should stimulate those attending to further study, both of the syllabus and of books dealing in greater detail with the questions raised. Classes should be regarded primarily as discussions serving these aims.

'Below, therefore, there is an outline for tutors aimed at helping them to take the classes on the basis of the "Question and Answer" method. Questions to be posed for discussion by tutors at classes are suggested. Tutors can, of course, add others or prepare a totally different set of questions. They should use these sessions and sections of sessions of the syllabus as material on which to base their replies.'

Then, underlined, it continues: 'It is of the greatest importance that tutors prepare the main lines of their reply beforehand, and not simply content themselves with posing the question.'

A model opening for classes based on a syllabus on 'Fundamental Principles of Marxism' is given in the Tutors' Guide for this series.

First, he should explain the method thus: 'We are going to use the "Question and Answer" method. This involves the tutor asking a question or questions around some major aspect of the problems dealt with in the syllabus. Then, after discussion on this is concluded the tutor sums up on this point. He then proceeds to the next problem in the same way. *To be successful this method requires maximum co-operation on the part of all comrades attending the class.* Therefore all comrades present are asked to participate as much as possible.'

Next, he moves on to outlining the ground that is to be covered during the particular session. The class members have been told that the syllabi which they have already been given should be studied both before and after classes and that the tutor will not necessarily try to deal with everything they contain. And so he continues: 'Tonight we will deal with problems arising from Session I of the syllabus: "Historical Materialism". We will be discussing mainly our view of historical development. What is the basis of human society, what makes society change, how classes arose and what caused this class struggle.

'The Marxist view of social development is the application to human history of the Marxist view of the world and of nature. We call this view dialectical materialism, which is the essence of Marxist philosophy. We begin, therefore, with a short discussion on some of the principles of Marxist philosophy.' That is all. From there he moves straight on to questions.

The first suggested in the Tutors' Guide is 'What is philosophy?' and then as subsidiaries, 'What do we mean by "materialism" and "idealism" in philosophy?' and 'Why do we call Marxist philosophy *dialectical* materialism?' and then, 'What are some aspects of the dialectical method?'

Very few, if any, of those attending the class will have any previous experience of philosophy. It is obvious, therefore, that they will be unable to answer such questions unless they have done the suggested reading. But if, on the contrary, they have done their little bit of homework well, then they will feel very proud, and perhaps somewhat superior, when they come up with the correct answers. After all, ordinary mortals rarely have even the first clue to what is dialectical materialism. Even to be able with any justification at all to call oneself a dialectical materialist is to appear to become part of an intellectual élite.

And so the questions go on. It is all very basic, but

81

immensely important in the making of a Communist leader. Terms are defined at every point. But the definitions given to ordinary terms are the Communists' own, not those normally accepted by others. Henceforth, as a consequence, the instructed Communist has his own private language. When he does his propaganda he uses words with which his hearers are already familiar. But as he utters them, or writes them, they mean one thing to him and something quite different to the non-Communists who receive them.

A good example of this is the series of questions which the tutor is recommended to ask at the end of this first session on 'Fundamental Principles of Marxism'. They go like this:

What is a class?
When did classes arise?
What is the class struggle?
What is the basis for the class struggle?
What is a revolutionary class?
What have been—and are—the major revolutionary classes in history?

By the time all those questions have been satisfactorily answered those attending the session will have learned quite a lot of Marxism—not just in a purely theoretical way, but on the basis of examples given out by class members themselves, and taken from industrial disputes in which they have been involved, tenants' agitations which the Communist Party has run, and so on. But also a new idea of what constitutes a class will have been accepted. It is such that those who have accepted it will reject automatically as so much hostile propaganda any suggestion that, for example, new classes of 'haves' and 'have nots' are now emerging, or could ever emerge in any circumstances, in Russia or in the other countries where the Communist Party is now the ruling power.

A document prepared by the Party Education Department has this to say about this method: 'The "Question and Answer" method in its extreme form consists in constructing the whole session around a series of questions. The tutor takes a minimum of time to start off and gives his contribution through his summaries to the answers to the questions. This method is most effective with a really small class, like a Branch class of four or five.

'Once again the method necessitates an even greater preparation than the straight lecture or "controlled discussion".'

Then comes this warning: 'A tutor needs to take great care (1) to get the right questions (2) to work out the answers to the questions *before* the class (3) to summarise the discussions, using the students' contribution as far as possible.'

In fact, the Education Department very conveniently takes care of both the questions and the answers for him. The average tutor is a busy man, and since the teaching of Marxism is surrounded by pitfalls which include the possibility of teaching heresy, he is most likely to take all the questions, just as they stand, from his 'Tutors' Guide'. And he is equally likely to take the answers. These are provided for him in the form of references to specific sentences in various Communist 'classics' and textbooks which he, as a tutor, will already possess.

A lot of thought has gone into both questions and answers. Often the questions are framed in such a way as, almost in passing, to undermine the position hitherto held and accepted unquestioningly by the new recruit who has come to the Party from some other section of the labour and socialist movement. Typical is the following taken from a 'Tutors' Guide':

'Tutor introduces: "We are going to discuss the question of the State—one of the most important questions, yet one in which there has been great lack of understanding in the British Labour movement. . . ."' And then he goes straight into a succession of questions which together present the Marxist definition of the State, which is contrary to that normally accepted by leaders and members of the British Labour movement. One has only to outline it to reveal the purely Marxist concept which is by this means implanted in the mind of the earnest recruit receiving instruction. It goes like this:

It is, of course, quite wrong to suppose that the State is 'neutral' and above classes. The State is, and must always be so long as classes continue, a weapon of the ruling class. Thus the capitalist State is organised in the interest of the capitalists as a class. Its task is to maintain and perpetuate capitalist society. This includes all its 'weapons of persuasion', such as the educational system, the Press, the pulpit, broadcasting and television, etc. Held in reserve but ever-present, ready for use, are the State's 'weapons of coercion' which include the judiciary, the police and in the last resort the armed forces. All serve the capitalist class by means of the so-called 'neutral' State.

It follows from this that it is right and proper that, in the socialist countries where the Communist Party rules, the State serves the new ruling class. This consists of the workers and toilers generally. Like the capitalist State, the proletarian State is a weapon of the ruling class—the new one, the proletariat. Communists are doing no more than every ruling class of history has done when they use the educational system, the Press, the pulpit, broadcasting and television, the judiciary, the police and in the last resort the armed forces in order to perpetuate the existing social system and to crush those who would make an end of it.

But there is this difference: all the capitalist cant has

been cut out. Whereas the capitalists hypocritically teach children in the schools and the public generally that the State is 'neutral' and attack all those who seek to expose this pretence, the Communists are open, frank and honest, declaring for all to hear that the State is a weapon of the ruling class. The poor have come into their own when at last, with a certain rough justice, the State is, with no apologies, used on their behalf and against their former oppressors.

If one assumes an almost total lack of knowledge of political theory on the part of those who are taught this, and remember that they have gone, in receptive mood, to learn rather than argue, then one can understand why such basic Marxist theories are accepted as revelations, insights into the world as it really is.

The majority doing the course have almost certainly never given very much thought to what constitutes a class or what is the nature of the State. But, by the time they have finished answering the questions, they will probably have no doubt about either. The definitions which have in any case been given, or suggested to them already in the printed syllabus, will seem self-evident.

In Communist countries, particularly in the early days after the Communists have seized power, indoctrination may be nakedly coercive. It is often quite openly a brain-washing process. In non-Communist countries it does not look like indoctrination at all. All the emphasis in guides to tutors is upon creating a friendly, co-operative atmosphere. There are no obvious pressures put upon those who take the Party's courses.

One guide for tutors deals with this under the some-what quaint heading 'Against "bashism" as a method of education'. This is explained as follows:

'There is an old diehard theory that the best way to teach children to swim is to throw them into the sea. All

85

the reports of miraculously floating infants are dutifully recorded. There is silence on those that sank.

'A similar theory once prevailed in certain circles of Party tutors that the way to teach people was to "bash" them. Publicly expose their weaknesses, misformulations and deviations. This may have had a good effect on some hardened characters but of those who never returned to be bashed again there is no record.'

The passage that follows may surprise those who have learned only of Communists and Communism from the anti-Communist propagandists and who therefore suppose the Communists' methods are always and necessarily ruthless and coercive.

'My own experience is that a kindly and decent attitude to students is one of the first demands on a tutor. Many comrades find things difficult; many are diffident, are nervous at first in the field of study. I am for the most co-operative and comradely atmosphere; an endeavour to listen patiently to what comrades have to say even if you feel it is wrong; an effort to pick out from contributions what is good as well as what is bad, and to explain mistakes in the most comradely and helpful manner. In general there is a very strong case for *modesty* on the side of tutors who often have less experience than those they are helping to study.

'Rough treatment should be reserved for those who are arrogant and intolerant to others in the course of the class or discussion.'

In practice, in non-Communist countries, the Party has learned that the subtle approach usually achieves far more than all the 'bashing'. In Communist hands the subtle method may take on an almost sinister quality, as ideas which would otherwise be unacceptable are skilfully got into the heads of those who attend the classes.

Such instruction leads those who are indoctrinated in

86

this way to abandon and repudiate practically all their past thinking and, indeed, to abandon the very things which first brought them to Communism. For example, the man who joined because he was at heart a pacifist comes in time quite naturally and 'logically' to accept the need for violence, for civil war and insurrection (even though anyone who has experienced civil wars knows that these tend to be much nastier and bloodier even than ordinary 'imperialist' wars) and to sit up till midnight studying Lenin on the art of insurrection as a means of establishing a system of society in which war will for ever-more be impossible.

The man with a liberal past comes believing that by joining the Communist Party he is somehow putting himself on the side of liberty, freedom, equality. After attending a few Marxist classes he has come to 'realise' that these are but 'bourgeois concepts' which must be not only abandoned but also combated, since they are all part of the means by which an inhuman social system is made acceptable, in the guise of being tolerant and democratic, to those who suffer at its hands.

And the man who has gone to Communism because he has always been on the side of reform, and for this reason has supported charitable causes and movements for social reform, is led to a point where he will accept Lenin's dictum that 'the Marxist is interested in reforms only so far as they may be used as stepping-stones to revolution'.

Says *Some Hints for Party Tutors*: 'What can be more important, what can be more rewarding, to help working class people to understand, in a *true* way, the world about them, than helping them to win a working class outlook and to shed the false ideas and values of monopoly capitalism.'

The use of these methods of instruction has proved

87

rewarding to the Communist Party. They stand up to what is the only real test for the Communist: they work. They achieve their end. There are lessons to be learned from them by non-Communists. One of the most important, to those who are themselves concerned with trying to achieve dedication and to produce leaders, is that an enormous amount of thought, time and trouble is put into Communist classes by all concerned. Both teacher and taught are made to feel that somewhere higher up in the organisation are people who *care*.

If the Soviet Union carries through a policy switch, new classes are organised in Communist Parties all over the world in order to explain it and demonstrate that it grows naturally out of Marxist-Leninist teachings. The same syllabi are often used, translated into a great variety of different languages, in Communist parties in scores of different countries. The same 'tutors' notes' are used, too. And before very long Moscow's Foreign Languages Publishing House is producing some new selection of Lenin's writings to support all this. A fairly recent example was when in all the newly-developing countries a new emphasis was to be put on the need for Worker-Peasant Alliances. This was supported by a specially-produced, handsomely-bound and low-priced volume composed of carefully selected writings by Lenin on the subject. Many more such examples might be given.

We find much the same at the lower, national level too. A more or less random example may be taken from the Communist Party members' publication *World News* of September 8, 1962, in which Jack Cohen of the Party's Education Department had an article.

The summer holiday season was over, or soon would be, and this meant new opportunities for work by Communist Party members. The Party was going to go all out to increase its membership before the next Party Congress.

It was preparing new campaigns against fascism, for peace, against Britain's entry into the Common Market. The writer was, from the Communist Party members' point of view, stating the obvious when he said that all these campaigns would be more effective 'if the fundamental, social and political factors are constantly explained. And this can only be done effectively on the principles of Marxism-Leninism'. More classes with more people attending them were, therefore, required at once.

'The coming autumn and winter,' he wrote, 'will be a time of mounting struggle, but in order to be effective, it must also be a time of study—study of the theoretical principles which guide our day-to-day work in the class struggle, in the fight for peace, democracy and socialism.'

The development of Marxist education within the Party had been discussed by the Executive Committee, which had adopted a detailed education plan for the following year, which Jack Cohen went on to explain. Many new classes, which he listed, were to be organised. These were aimed at every category of Party worker from the rawest recruit to the well-instructed cadre. Special material was already being prepared to back them up. There would be simple introductory lectures. The Party press would carry regular educational articles 'of especial interest to our new members'. All branches would be organising a wide variety of classes which would include 'day and weekend schools on a branch basis'.

There would also be a national campaign of public lectures to which 'our best lecturers and tutors will be allocated', aimed at spreading Communist ideas among the general public.

'A basic aim of education is encouragement of personal study—a practice neglected by too many active comrades on the grounds that they have "no time".

'To overcome this mistaken view we are launching a

89

scheme, especially amongst our newer members, to make available a basic library of Marxist-Leninist books.' In addition, a *Reader's Guide to the Study of Marxism-Leninism* was being made available.

This is typical Communist thinking and planning. A new political situation, a new campaign, a turn in policy —all these call automatically for more study, directly related to the new development. The Communist is a dialectical materialist. He believes that despite the conflict of opposites, he must in his own life find a unity of opposites too. In the work of organisation and in his own personal political life he must unite the apparent opposites of theory and practice. If he achieves this, then he becomes a fully integrated Communist, fully integrated as a person, too. And the Party is only being truly Marxist when its campaigns are backed by study, and its studies are linked to campaigns.

In an article entitled 'Studying Marxism-Leninism', in the *World Marxist Review* of December, 1964, Sebastian Calderón describes how the illegal Communist Party of Guatemala, of which he is a leader, is organising the 'political education' of its members in underground conditions and in the face of 'police persecution'. Classes include ones which deal with the country's economy, history, class structure. A small handbook has been produced which explains for semi-literates the terms they will hear used at their study classes. Pamphlets and syllabi using only the simplest language have been prepared. Activists from the capital have been assigned, to 'help with the discussions' in the rural branches.

The British Party Education Department not long ago dealt with the problem of the worker with little education who comes tired, at the end of the day, to classes and then is told that he must do some 'basic' reading if he is to understand it. It suggested that where possible one com-

rade who had a background of better Marxist education
should be assigned, to help such people. This will be his
major Party responsibility. He should, if required, be
prepared to sit at the side of the tired worker as he reads,
explaining sentence by sentence, almost word by word,
what is being read. This, it points out, is not an extrava-
gant use of personnel. If at the end of one year's such
activity a new Marxist leader has been developed, it has
been well worth while.

It will not, incidentally, be easy to persuade such a
worker, if the guide and mentor has done his job properly,
that this is some sinister process of brain-washing. On the
contrary his reply when such a charge is made is likely
to be: 'Who else in this world ever showed so much interest in helping a poor so-and-so like me?'

* * * * *

To understand more fully what all this emphasis upon
constant and relevant instruction means in the life of the
Party, one may legitimately, I think, draw a parallel with
the Catholic Church.

New policies, new approaches to old questions (some of
which to the outsider may look curiously like the 'somer-
saults' of which the Communists are accused) have
emerged from the deliberations of the Fathers attending
the Second Vatican Council. In the main, the laity and,
for that matter, to a somewhat lesser extent, the clergy,
have got their knowledge of these things from the secular
press. For some, many of the ideas and 'directives' which
have come from the Council have been bewildering. The
obedience of some of the older priests has been sorely
tried; the new atmosphere of greater freedom has led to
the emergence of what some of the conservative element
fearfully regard as a potentially anti-clerical if not heretical
trend among sections of the educated laity.

91

If the Communists were confronted with a similar situation, and if the Church was the Communist Party, then the Catholic hierarchy of any particular country would immediately appoint a commission of the best brains to determine how all this might be explained to the whole of the faithful—providing them with the fullest and deepest possible understanding of what was being done and the reasons for it.

Then classes would be organised within every organisation in the Church, with the tutors first doing special courses at which the method of presentation would be discussed as well as the content of what was going to be taught.

Someone would be responsible for listing the 'required reading' and this would be cut down to an absolute minimum so that it was limited to what was directly relevant to the subjects under discussion. Syllabi would be prepared, printed and distributed.

The study courses would be aimed at every group within the Church, from the least educated to the most highly, from the rawest new convert to the professor of theology.

When the classes were held, priests would learn how their work would be affected by the various Vatican Council decrees and how this might be got over to the people through the pulpit, in instruction classes and in normal pastoral activities. Teaching nuns and religious would have their own syllabi, and classes at which their work would be reviewed in the light of the new trends— and related at every turn to their practical, day-to-day activities as well as to their devotional life. Members of organisations for choristers and altar servers would discuss how their activities would be affected by the changes in the liturgy.

Catholic trade unionists and others involved in social

action would attend classes at which their role in the new 'dialogue with the world' and the new and better relations with non-Catholic Christians and others would be discussed. Organisations for Catholic students, graduates, intellectuals would have the job of taking a new look at past, present and future approaches to those amongst whom they worked and with whom they associated, so that the latter too might play their full and very important part in the dialogue with the world—at their own level.

All this may or may not be practicable. What seems certain is that if it was carried through with any degree of success at all, it could lead only to Catholics being immensely more interested in their Catholicism, far better equipped to apply their Christianity to their daily life in the secular world, and it might well lead to a tremendous renewal of the life of all the 'people of God' who collectively make up the Church.

The Church is not organised in this way. This is not 'how Catholics do things'. But to note this difference between the Church and the Communist Party is to be given just one more insight into why it is that the Communists, whom Catholics describe as 'the children of this world', so often appear to make a greater impact on our time, despite the relative smallness of their numbers, and why, to the mystification of many Christians, they so often are clearly more deeply committed, more single-minded than the Christians themselves.

In what we have seen of Communist 'education' and tutorial methods, it will be clear that there is much that the non-Communist, and particularly the Christian, may not copy. There is much in it that will, quite properly, be an affront to the mind of any democrat. But there is much, also, from which others might learn. This is particularly true of the Communists' *attitude* to the question of study

93

and formation, and their recognition that those who would serve a cause must establish a unity of theory and practice in their own lives. It is here that the non-Communists tend most often to be at their weakest. It is assuredly where the Communists have their greatest strength.

CHAPTER VII

'You Must be the Best'

IN the years since 1948, when I left the Communists and became a Catholic, I have heard perhaps half a dozen sermons which have made a deep impression on me, perhaps just one or two I shall never forget. One of the unforgettable ones was preached on an Easter Sunday morning in a church on the edge of a South-East Asian jungle.

I was living as a political detainee at the time in the near-by local jail, and one of the guards, a Muslim, had been ordered to take me in the prison van to Mass. These circumstances, no doubt, helped to fix the occasion in my memory in a special way. But more particularly, it was the simple effectiveness of the sermon itself which indelibly imprinted it on my mind.

The sermon had already just begun when I arrived. An old Indian priest was preaching to a congregation of Indians and Chinese the majority of whom were very poor. He told them that the women on the first Easter Sunday went looking in the garden for the risen Lord. They looked in the tomb, and they did not find Him there. They looked around the garden; again they could not find Him. But, said the preacher, 'you do not have to look in a tomb, you do not have to look around a garden to find the risen Lord. He is in your hands. When you go out to work tomorrow, whether you are riding a trishaw, or digging a drain or whatever you may be doing as your daily work, you will be co-operating in God's work of creation. God is in your hands.'

Sitting in front of me was an old Indian coolie with gnarled, bare legs around which varicose veins entwined themselves like creepers on the branch of a tree. Those who know the Orient will be familiar with his type. As the preacher said the words 'God is in your hands', I saw the old man look at his toil-worn, calloused, twisted hands, and broken nails, almost in awe. Something tremendous was happening to him. One could watch a great yet simple truth enter his consciousness. Recognition of it spread across his face, which took on a look of sheer wonderment. Throughout the rest of the sermon he looked, time after time, at the hands which had suddenly taken on a new, sublime significance. It is my guess that his work, whatever it was, would never be the same for him again. Suddenly, no matter how degraded that work might be, it became meaningful for him. His Christianity suddenly became relevant to his work. Or, to turn it round the other way, his work was suddenly linked to his beliefs so that God and religion would no longer belong just to Mass on Sunday. His beliefs could be related to cleaning the monsoon drains the next day, or pedalling away from morning till night on a heavy trishaw.

That, of course, is how any Christian should see his work. This is one of those obvious things. But it is not necessarily how Christians do see it. If they did, the so-called 'Christian West' would be very different from what it is. The values of Sunday Mass or Service would be taken to the Stock Exchange, the board meeting, the marketing campaign office, the factory, but quite evidently, they normally are not. For the Christian, and for most others, work is divorced from belief. This is not true of the Communist.

The Communists' approach to work comes in one sense much nearer to that of the old Indian preacher. For them, their place of work provides them with an ideal opportunity of doing a job for Communism. The Communist sees it like this: It is in the nature of capitalist society to bring increasingly large numbers of people into daily contact with each other in order to produce the goods, and therefore the profits, which the capitalist employers demand. This is one of the means by which the capitalist class digs its own grave—it cannot escape from doing so, no matter how it may try. For, by bringing together ever-larger numbers of workpeople into ever-larger factories, the capitalist class presents the Communists in them with a ready-made audience. From the Communist's point of view, they are by the nature of things obliged to provide him with a golden opportunity for disseminating his ideas amongst large numbers of workpeople.

You may announce and organise a public meeting and if you work sufficiently hard, perhaps for weeks and months on end and, if you have a good or well-known speaker, you may be able to get together an audience of 5,000 people. If you do, you will probably consider that you have had more than usual success. But capitalist society presents the Communist with, maybe, scores of thousands of people as a ready-made audience, not just once, but every day. This audience is presented to him free, at the enemy's expense. The capitalists provide the building, they get the people together and give him the opportunity to be with them for six, seven, maybe eight or more hours a day. He stands amongst them at his machine as they work, he eats with them in the canteen at lunchtime, chats with them during the morning and afternoon tea breaks.

The most important part of the Communist's day is, or should be, that which he spends at work. He see his work as giving him a wonderful opportunity to do a job

97

for the cause. By way of contrast, the average Catholic Actionist feels that his time for going into action on behalf of his beliefs begins after he has returned from his day's work, had a meal, changed and has just an hour or two left—when he is already tired—to give to his cause.

The Communists, having decided that the ruling class has providentially provided them with this opportunity, set about exploiting it in an organised way.

With a good deal of justification, they reason that you are most likely to be effective if you are respected. In an industry in which skilled craftsmen are employed, or in a profession, you will be respected if you are good at your job—not just because you are good at talking about your beliefs. It may be quite irrational, but the fact is that, if you are recognised as being outstanding on one thing, you will be listened to on all sorts of subjects in no way related to it.

This is particularly true in the case of the worker employed in an industry where there are still men who take a pride in their craft. Craftsmen respect a good craftsman, just as businessmen, with perhaps less justification, respect a successful businessman. In motor- and aircraft-engineering, in shipbuilding and a whole range of other skilled occupations, a man is viewed with contempt by the better workers if he is known to be poor at his job. He is a no-good, a bum. As a consequence, they are unlikely to listen to him receptively when he talks on other subjects. This may be a barrier which he can overcome, as some have done, but it is a very real barrier indeed.

And so, the Communists say, if you are going to be really effective in your place of work, you must set out to be the best man at your job. In many Communist parties this has even been made an unwritten rule. It is repeated in Communist circles over and over again—every member

should aim to be the best man at his job. It is not a bad
rule.

I knew a man who helped to lead a movement of the
unemployed from just after the end of World War I right
through to the beginning of World War II. When there was
an unemployed agitation in South Wales he would be
there to help build it up. Barricades went up in the streets
on Merseyside and he would arrive to lead the fight. If
hunger marchers went to London he would go with them.
He was a full-time agitator, devoting all his efforts to
spreading Communism amongst the unemployed by
championing their cause. As a result of riots in which he
was involved, he went to both jail and hospital time after
time.

By the time World War II came, most of the unemployed
had already been absorbed into war industries. There were
less and less of them for him to organise. Then came the
certainty that able-bodied men would be directed by
Government either into the armed forces or into industry.
The Party leaders decided that he should return volun-
tarily to industry instead of waiting to be directed there.

During World War I he had worked in a branch of
engineering which required a very high degree of skill. He
decided to go back to the same type of work. By way of
preparation he dug out and studied his engineering
manuals again. Then he applied for, and got, a job in a
factory engaged in war work, employing top-grade craftsmen. The workers there had never been particularly well
known for their Communist sympathies. When they heard
that the notorious agitator was coming to work among
them they were cynical. 'He may be all right at talking,
and leading unemployed, and fighting the police at the
barricades, but we'll soon see whether he's any good at
his job,' they said.

He arrived on the job and, contrary to expectations, he

did not talk, he did not agitate. He just got on with the work. And, for a period of some months, that is all he did. During that time he concentrated on recapturing his old skill, mastering the work once more. He was an intelligent man, the old skill returned, and, more than this, he established a reputation as a top-grade craftsman. His workmates began to see him in a new light. Throughout this period he played no leading role in the workshop nor in his trade union branch. He attended factory meetings, participated in the election of shop stewards, attended his trade union branch meetings, but simply as a rank and filer.

Only when he had already, to the surprise of everyone, established himself as a craftsman amongst craftsmen did he go into action. By this time he had the respect of every worker in the factory and in the trade union branch. It was only then that he stood for a vacancy on the shop stewards' committee. He was elected. In his trade union branch he let his name go forward for a minor position and got it. He did both jobs well. Before long his was the dominant influence in the shop stewards' committee. Simultaneously, he went up the trade union ladder. Within two years of returning to an industry from which he had been absent for twenty years, he had obtained one of the most influential positions in his union, where he could profoundly influence policies which concerned the working lives and conditions of hundreds of thousands of Britain's key war-workers.

The Communist approach to the choice of methods to be used, or rejected, where no Marxist principles as such are involved, is the pragmatic one. They test their methods by the simple question 'Does it work?' They have demonstrated that being the best man at your job does work very well indeed. They have proven this over and over again.

They know that, because of all that has been said and written against Communism and because of certain features of Communism itself, what they have to offer, what they are trying to 'sell' the public, is not immediately acceptable. They have to overcome prejudice or, if you like, 'sales resistance'. The individual member working inside a factory learns that he can most quickly overcome this difficulty by quietly establishing a reputation for being a good craftsman and a good trade unionist. This is a tip worth taking for anyone who is trying to put across unpopular ideas, or who is a member of an unpopular minority seeking to activise an apathetic majority.

This same rule is applied to the Communists' work among students. As is well known, Communists are active amongst students everywhere—this is particularly true today of Asia, Africa and Latin America. It is true that you will find the occasional Communist student who gets so carried away by his Communism, gives so much time to political activity, that he fails all his examinations. This is not viewed with approval by the Party. Indeed, he is likely to be called to account for it. His Party group leader is likely to tell him: 'You work very hard for the cause, and we are very grateful to you for what you have done. But you would have done a better job for Communism if you had passed your examinations instead of failing them. You would be more likely to carry conviction amongst your fellow students. More important, you would be more effective later on. You will not always be a student. Student life is a preparation for what follows. We want you to use this student period as your preparation for going out and making a mark in your profession so that you may do a good job for Communism there. So the better you do in your exams, the better it will be for the cause.'

Once the student has grasped this point, his studies become more meaningful. They cease to be just a wearisome necessity and become a form of activity for the cause. If he finds them hard or distasteful, then this is a sacrifice he is making. Such an approach to his studies tends to make him more successful in them.

The Communists carry this same unwritten rule that each member should be the best of his group into their activities in other organisations.

I well remember hearing William Gallacher, a day or two after his election as a member of parliament in 1931, remind us at a meeting in Manchester that the Communist 'must always be the best member of any organisation to which he belongs. . . . I am going to try to be the best man in the House of Commons,' he said. 'I want my constituents in West Fife to come to believe that they have the very best M.P., one who looks after their interests better than anyone else can do.'

William Gallacher was not one of Parliament's great orators. His excessively broad Scots accent made most of what he said quite incomprehensible to those who stayed in the Chamber to hear him. But he became a first-rate M.P., nonetheless, as anyone who spent any time in his constituency would be obliged to admit.

The views he expressed in the Chamber, even when they were understood, were abhorrent to most of those who heard him. There was little likelihood that he would make any converts there, or even that he would be able to build up around himself any significant number of sympathisers. But back in his constituency, amongst the mining population who had returned him to Westminster, he could be uncrowned king—by working night and day for them. And this is what he did.

At the end of a week in Parliament he travelled hundreds of miles to his remote constituency. There throughout the weekend he made himself available to anyone who wanted his help, no matter whether they were Communists or anti-Communists, Labour, Liberal or Conservative, Atheist like himself, Scots Presbyterians, or—as a very high proportion of them were—Catholics. He would take up their problems with one government department after another, keep on worrying at them like a terrier with a rag, give Ministers and civil servants no peace until he had got the answers he needed. It was not his performance in the debating Chamber which got this Communist fighter returned to Parliament time after time by people, the majority of whom were anti-Communists. It was the simple fact that he saw that the only way which he could be 'the best M.P.' was by putting himself completely at their disposal and working for them behind the scenes.

Of course, this approach is not exclusive to the Communists. When I think of some of the best missionaries I have seen in action, I recall men who have brought much the same approach to their work.

I think, for example, of when I was staying, early in 1962, with a group of Jesuits in Calcutta. Among them were two Belgians who, in advance of Pope John XXIII and Pope Paul VI, were already conducting a fruitful 'dialogue' with non-Christians. This was made possible by the approach they brought to their work. One had earned a reputation in Indian academic circles for being one of the foremost Bengali scholars in East Bengal. The other, a Sanskrit scholar, is particularly known for having mastered Indian classical music. This leads to his frequently being invited to attend Hindu marriages, weddings and funerals in order to sing Sanskrit hymns, of his own composition, addressed to the Holy Ghost or the Blessed Trinity. These men have the entrée to circles which would otherwise be closed to them, a world of culture in which they could

103

play no part, were it not for the fact that they, too, have set out to be the best men at the job.

They have not gone out to crudely proselytise: they have not thrust their religion down other peoples' throats. But they have contributed to the thought of serious, cultured people interested in ideas. They are not hunting for converts like a Red Indian hunting for scalps. But one may be sure that, if any come, they will not be second-class people.

Such men as those Belgian Jesuits attract the best. In other words, they tend to attract people of their own type. This rule of the Communists, whether applied to work or to other activities, helps to ensure that the Party gets quality in its human material. It helps to explain why so often it is the best, not the worst, who go to Communism.

CHAPTER VIII

Campaigns, Criticism and Cadres

'THE Party lives by its campaigns.' This is one of its slogans and, unlike some others, it has a lot of truth in it. The majority of recruits to the Party, as noted earlier, come in through the campaigns which the Party organises. Campaigning keeps the Party members active the whole of the time. This is a deliberate policy. A lot of thought has to be given to ensuring that one campaign follows another almost non-stop. Communists, if they are worthy of the name at all, are always active. Activity in itself serves an important purpose, but it has to be made as meaningful as possible so that more and more non-Communists may be drawn into association with the Party.

For many people who are not Communists, activity is almost an end in itself. Years ago, I knew a man who devoted every moment of his spare time, seven days a week, 365 days a year, to raising and racing homing pigeons. Most of us know others who give the whole of their leisure to cultivating orchids or, may be, to playing bridge, bringing to these as serious an approach as any man ever brought to a cause that might change the world. Some spend their time organising other people.

In urging their members to be active, therefore, Communists are not going against the grain. They are using something which has its own appeal. People, once they are suitably activised, get satisfaction from being active. If this can be made meaningful, then they will get even greater satisfaction, for they will feel that they are engaged in something virtuous. The Communists recognise this. To an exceptional extent they succeed in keeping their people almost constantly in action and in making members' activity relevant to the needs or desires of the people they are seeking to influence and activise.

This, then, is their approach to the technique of campaigning. Collectively the leaders at all levels must find issues upon which to campaign which will relate activity to the real needs of the people. Ideally, these issues should be linked to the people's deepest desires. Quite frequently Communist campaigns have on the face of it little to do with the long-term aims of Communism. But they have a great deal to do with keeping Party members in action, attracting others to the movement and creating the image of a party which alone concerns itself with the lives and problems of ordinary folk.

Much of Mao Tse-tung's success, particularly during the guerilla phase of his fight, depended upon his party's ability to discover the needs of the people and to come before them as their champions. In one of his essays he describes this approach as 'from the people to the people'. By this he means that the Party should send its members out among the people, try to discover what they want most, what are the questions which are troubling their minds, what are the things which are nearest to their hearts. Then they should report back to their Party, cell or group what they have discovered. This should then be discussed and the means be found by which it can be used for the Communist cause. The Party then adapts its campaigns to the things the people already want. You take the raw material for campaigning from the people, give it a Communist content, then give it back to them again.

Since, as Mao notes, it originated with them, they will naturally respond to it.

The Communists say that their aim is a Communist world. That, as I have previously emphasised, means every country of the world. This aim is kept firmly in the Communist's mind the whole of the time. He is made to feel that whatever he is doing is related to that ultimate aim. He must never lose sight of this, or the campaigns may come to be an end in themselves. Or he may get so caught up in campaigning for reforms that he comes in time to believe that the existing society is capable of being reformed, whereas as a Marxist, he should believe that it must be swept away as a necessary precondition for the building of his Communist world.

Nonetheless, you cannot campaign exclusively and continuously for a Communist world. That is the long-term objective. Since by its very nature it is incapable of immediate achievement, people will before long grow weary of campaigning for it if they have no other objectives towards which to work.

Books by Lenin and Stalin read like military textbooks. The terminology is that of the military academy. Communists think in terms of strategy and tactics. They think like so many army officers. And any military man should know that the art of campaigning is to be able to maintain the morale of your troops come what may.

He knows that a big defeat may lead to his men's becoming demoralised, but that there are ways of avoiding this. He knows, or should do, that you can take a big defeat and still maintain morale if you throw your troops quickly into action again in some sector of the front where they can get a quick victory, no matter how small. Leave them inactive and before long they are demoralised. So, for this reason, you need your long-term objectives, but you need intermediate and short-term objectives as well. The long-term objective of a Communist world may not be achieved for some time (although Communists believe it will be achieved in our lifetime). But Communist Party members are also given goals which are capable of realisation here and now. Pie in the sky may have its own place, but men need something to keep them going in the meantime.

The Communist's intermediate goal is to win his own country for Communism. It is the national Party's task to devise ways and means of achieving this and to involve all its members in the job. Each Communist is, therefore, at one and the same time working for a Communist world and working to make his own particular country Communist as a contribution to the long-term goal.

It is unnecessary, here, I suppose, to mention that there is a certain similarity in this between the Communist and the Christian who wishes to win the world for Christ—his long-term aim—and to accomplish the Christianisation of the society in which he lives, which might be described as the intermediate one.

But there must also be the short-term, immediate objectives. Campaigning for these is like the little skirmishes into which the wise officer sends his men knowing in advance that they stand a good chance of getting a small victory. This is of great psychological importance in constantly keeping morale at the highest pitch. Campaigning for well chosen immediate objectives helps to ensure that members do not lose heart, it keeps them continuously working for the cause, and therefore tied to it. A sudden cessation of activity, due to sickness or some other contingency, has been the downfall of many a Communist—it has led to his attitude towards Communism cooling off and to his subsequent defection.

The immediate objective may be almost anything which links people with the Party, weakens the position of the 'ruling class' and the opponents of Communism, or advances the cause of Communism. If the members can see results from time to time, as Communists normally do, then they feel that all the fighting and campaigning is worth while, and they get the very human satisfaction of seeing 'something attempted, something done'.

One obvious immediate objective is the making of converts. This is something which is in the mind of the Communist all the time. He is out to make converts whenever and wherever he can. Often the methods of individual members have been crude. They have proselytised so blatantly that they have built up a very natural and understandable resistance to their efforts. This is not peculiar to Communists. There have been many others who have fallen into the same trap.

Communists learn from their mistakes and so their conversion methods have tended to become more subtle as the years have gone on. But this does not mean that their members have become less conversions-minded. Any Communist who is worth his salt, moving into association with a new group of people, will almost instinctively look around to see who are the 'probables', the ones who may most easily and usefully be brought into the Party. Having selected these, he will try to devise ways and means of bringing about their conversion. I did this myself years ago when I was a Communist. Some of my converts have by now left the Party, some are today working against Communism, but there are still many who are totally dedicated to the cause.

Whilst each individual Communist is expected to be on the lookout for converts the whole of the time, working patiently upon his workmates, friends and family, it is also recognised that the Party by means of its propaganda has the responsibility of trying to convert public opinion; to so change the climate of opinion that conversions will be brought about more easily.

What is of immediate interest to us is that the Party does succeed in creating in its members a certain attitude of mind. This is one which leads to their believing that they have got the best thing on earth. That, since this is so, they have a right and a responsibility to share it with others. By bringing converts into the Party they are helping to hasten the day when the Party's intermediate aim and, in due course, its long-term aim too, will be achieved.

The campaigns for short-term objectives are sometimes and undeniably in the interests of the common people—provided that we can forget the Communists' ulterior motive. A Communist rejoices when he learns of some unnecessary hardship which people are enduring and around which the Party can conduct an agitation. A quick and relatively easy success will improve the Party's image and will mean more new readers of the Communist Press, possibly so many converts to the Party, too.

A Communist must keep close to the people if he is to make his full contribution to the life of the Party. 'We are the fish, the people are the stream,' said Mao Tse-tung. By this he meant that Communists are so close to the people that they can sense every new current and act accordingly.

It may be that parents of young children in a particular neighbourhood are with good cause worried by the fact that a road, hitherto regarded as relatively safe for their children to cross, has now become dangerous. Or it may be that there is an inadequate transport service which makes it difficult for housewives to get to the shops or for workers to get to the station from which they commute. Whatever the issue may be, provided that it does not in some way conflict with the broader aims and intentions of the Party, the local branch may, once it has become aware of it, be expected to go into action.

I recall how on one occasion, back in my Communist

days, I discovered that people living on a housing estate just on the outskirts of the town where I was working, had to go some three-quarters of a mile out of their way in order to get into the town. This was because their way was blocked by the mainline railway which ran past the estate. I at once started a campaign for the construction of a footbridge over the railway. It was a perfectly legitimate demand—someone should have provided such a bridge years ago when the estate was first built. So far as I recall I got literally every resident to support the demand. A splendid agitation, with petitions, meetings and marches—and good Press publicity—was conducted in the name of the Communist Party.

We did not get our footbridge, but we got a unit of the Communist Party established on the estate, where previously I was the only member living there, and so, from our point of view, the campaign was a complete success.

No matter what the Communists' motives may be, the fact is that quite frequently the issues about which they campaign, and from which they get their converts, are ones about which others could and should be concerned. If Christians, democrats and others are out of touch with the people, if they do not see that they have a responsibility to concern themselves with the everyday needs of the common people, then they have no cause to complain when the Communists come along, conduct a campaign for their own purposes, take the converts and, maybe, the credit too.

*   *   *   *   *

Members of Catholic organisations in particular are often frustrated by the fact that at study classes and 'formation' courses they can discuss first principles and 'man's inalienable human rights' for as long as they please and everyone in authority is perfectly happy about them,

111

but, once they try to translate into action what they have learned, trouble begins. The clergy are nervous of what they may do and watch with apprehension as young people set out to try to apply their Christianity to some segment of the paganised society in which they live. So long as the laity are talking, it often seems, they are not likely to come to much harm but once they go out and start trying to do things, red lights begin to shine in the distance.

Sometimes they will organise ambitious and potentially useful local surveys. They go from house to house trying to discover what are the problems of young workers. It is all very purposeful, it has the appearance of being relevant. And then the gathering of information, the knocking on doors, the questioning and discussion comes to an end. The survey is completed. Some useful information has been collected. On paper, they know more than they did before about, say, the exploitation of apprentices as cheap labour in factories, the perpetuation of immoral 'initiation' rituals in workshops employing large numbers of women, the number of youngsters who never go inside a church and who live lives devoid of any purpose or direction or who keep themselves going night and day with purple heart pills.

And after that comes nothing except anti-climax. No form of remedial or preventive activity is embarked upon. The ground work has been laid for a campaign, but there is no campaign. Someone in the background who is answerable to his superiors is nervous where it might lead. This, over and over again, has led to a falling away in membership and activity of such excellent organisations as, for example, the Young Christian Workers.

This is not a problem for the Communists. Once more we are up against the paradox of those who are supposed to be the great champions of the human individual showing less faith in people than do the Communists who are supposed to be the enemies of the human person. Party members are sent into action and they go knowing that their superiors believe in them. The leaders send the rank and file into campaigns expecting that they will make mistakes, which of course they do. But they teach them also to learn from those mistakes.

The importance of the role of the laity—the need to consult them and to create personal and organisational links which will enable them to communicate with the clergy and hierarchy is beginning to be recognised as a result of the deliberations of the Second Vatican Council. But old attitudes and habits die hard. Too frequently, when Christian laymen go into action they do not feel that their leaders really believe in them. They do not feel that they have the confidence of the priest or Bishop as they launch into some campaign. There are reasons for this. The problem is not a simple one. But it is very real, particularly to those who find themselves frustrated by what appears to be an almost total lack of trust. Laymen see priests make mistakes time after time and fervently hope that they are learning from them. They, also, want to be able to run the risk of making mistakes—and to be given the chance of learning from these too.

I recall how on one occasion I had lectured to a large gathering of Catholic trade unionists. The meeting had by any standard been a success. But later, over a quiet meal together, the priest told me: 'You have got my people all wanting to go into action, but my hair is going to stand on end. I do not know what they are going to say or do in the factory. I do not know what sort of heresies they are going to be guilty of.'

If you never say a word on behalf of your beliefs, if you never do anything, you are never going to be guilty of heresy—except that the total failure to do anything about your beliefs seems to me almost to constitute a heresy in itself. Perhaps it is one of the greatest and most deadly heresies of our time.

Of course there is a calculated risk involved in sending a man into action. There may be losses and failures. I have travelled the world too much not to know that priests going out to the missions are not infrequently involved in emotional crises in the first months of their life abroad and so are quickly recalled to the home base. No one suggests that for this reason priests and religious should be withdrawn from the missions. When the same happens to lay missionaries who go off to distant places, there is still too often someone in authority who concludes that the modern lay mission effort is a menace—and who possibly bans henceforth all lay missionaries from his diocese. Yet human beings make mistakes, and anyone who is in charge of others has to learn to be prepared to see those mistakes made.

Any Communist will say that the important thing is not that mistakes are made but that people must be taught to learn from them. They have demonstrated that they can often learn more directly from their failures than from their successes. This is one reason why, although Communists, from the top world leaders downwards, obviously make mistakes it is exceptional for them to make the same mistake twice—and I do not mean that they are all banished or demoted like Mr. Molotov or Mr. Khrushchev. This, today, is reserved in the main for top leaders. Our Western statesmen make their mistakes too, but, one fears, they go on making the same ones for years on end.

It is not by coincidence that this happens. We paper over our mistakes. This is a form of hypocrisy, of downright dishonesty, even though it is done very frequently in the name of courtesy. The Communists, on the other hand, are ruthlessly critical of themselves and of each

114

other. They do not have to bother about practising Christian charity.

Nevertheless, there is something to be learned from their self-critical approach. It is a wonderful antidote to complacency. They call it 'Bolshevik self-criticism', which sounds like a piece of Communist jargon but is very meaningful to the Communists. They would certainly claim that it is one of the healthiest and best institutions in the Party's life.

They run a campaign, engage in some form of activity, and this is followed by what is called the 'inquest'. At the inquest they are not concerned about being polite to each other. Their sole concern is to discover what weaknesses were revealed by the campaign, what mistakes they made. So they do not tell each other how wonderful everyone was and how splendidly the campaign was run. On the contrary.

When you make a contribution to the discussion, you first criticise yourself, admitting that it was in such-and-such a way that you went wrong. You make no reference to your successes. These can be taken for granted. Instead you say: 'I slipped up completely on this, on that and on the other.' Then, having criticised yourself honestly and frankly, you consider you are entitled to do the same with the other people present.

You point out where they went wrong, too, and seek the views of others on the matter. Every mistake is brought to the surface. But, more important, persistent probing reveals why the mistakes were made, how they might have been avoided and how the lessons learned from them can be applied to specific forms of activity which are already planned.

Their language is perhaps more severe and sharp than that which the Christian may legitimately use. But the critical approach is a good one for any organisation which takes its work as seriously as does the Communist party, and which considers itself to be, or aspires to be, an élite and which is anxious to be just as effective as possible.

Certainly for the Communists' purposes, they have demonstrated that the idea is a good one. One of its most important consequences is that the leaders feel free to send members into action without being inhibited by the thought that they may make mistakes. For they already know that mistakes need not be disastrous, provided that all concerned study them in due course, learn from them and try to ensure that they are not repeated. Bolshevik self-criticism is of considerable psychological importance because it helps to create a serious-minded approach to the members' activities. To the man who joins the Communist Party and sees self-criticism at work it looks like clear evidence that here is a serious-minded group of people anxious to cut through all the cant and nonsense and get on with jobs that matter.

Let me give you from my own experience an example of the way it works. At the beginning of the last war, I was living in an industrial suburb in London. The population of the town had almost doubled in, I think it was, the previous six years. Since it was surrounded by built-up areas and there was no undeveloped land within the town's boundaries, this meant that there had to be two families living in almost every house. The accommodation for domestic fuel, which had been provided by the builders of the houses was naturally intended for the needs of one family, not two. This was bound to create a problem.

But the problem became immensely greater when Britain had to change from a peace-time economy to a war economy. Everything was diverted to meet the needs of the war factories. This included coal. In many parts of

Britain there was, as a consequence, a domestic-fuel crisis. The coal did not get to the domestic consumer, it went to the factories instead, and, in addition, the railways were kept clear for the movement of raw material required by industry.

At that time, I was working on the staff of the *Daily Worker* and so most of my activities and interests were in Central London. I saw little of my home borough which had become little more than a dormitory for me. But in time I became aware that it was in the throes of a severe fuel crisis. No domestic coal had come there for weeks. The people were not of the class, nor had they the facilities, to lay in large stocks in advance. So they had already used up their fuel. The winter was a bitterly cold one. People were living in their unheated homes and this involved discomfort for a great many, actual suffering for some.

I became aware of all this when I found that I had no coal left myself. I called together the leaders of the local Communist Party. 'There is a fuel crisis which is already hitting the working class of this town really hard,' I said. 'People are suffering. You are living here, most of you are working here, you must have known about it, and yet you have done nothing. The question is, what are we going to do in this situation? This calls for action by the Party.'

I sat down there and then and wrote a leaflet which declared that the townspeople would 'refuse to shiver in silence'. I described the situation in which old people sat by empty stoves and sick people died in unheated homes. Fuel, I wrote, should have been brought to the homes of people and must be, immediately.

At that stage of the war, we Communists were opposing the war effort. We had said that this was an unjust war and our political line was to try and undermine it. A campaign to have fuel diverted to the homes of the people would, we knew, in its own small way hit the war effort.

117

But it was also concerned with the needs of the people. This was an ideal combination.

The leaflet ended by calling on housewives to go to the town hall on Thursday afternoon at 3 o'clock and make their anger known. We had practically no housewives in the Party branch and so could have no idea what the response would be. But I told the local leaders to have 10,000 copies of the leaflet printed, distribute them, and we would see who turned up.

The most we dared hope for was that sufficient people would come along for us to be able to have a fairly typical Communist deputation—five genuine working-class housewives and Douglas Hyde to keep them on the Party line—which would interview the Mayor. At the appointed time we went along to see what results, if any, the leaflet had brought.

There was, in fact, no question of getting some small deputation elected from those who were there. Thousands of angry housewives had come along to let the world know that they were not prepared to shiver in silence. I have been in civil wars, I have been in revolutions, but I have never seen anything more frightening than thousands of angry housewives demanding fuel to warm their shivering children. They stormed the town hall, they chased the Mayor out of his parlour, then went off to the fuel office and did the same with the fuel officer. They broke some windows. Then they went home.

On the following Sunday morning I was awakened early by the sound of heavy trucks going up and down the street where I was living and, by the sound of it, up and down all the neighbouring streets too. I pulled back my blackout curtains, peeped outside and saw that even the garbage disposal men had been pressed by the local authority into delivering coal. The Council had mobilised practically every available truck in the place.

Our housewives' demonstration had been given front-page treatment by the *Daily Worker* which described it as a great Communist campaign. It goes without saying that Monday's *Daily Worker* carried an even bigger story, with bolder headlines, proclaiming the great victory for which our local Communist Party had been responsible. And the appropriate moral was underlined that the people of that London industrial suburb were now no longer shivering, because they had refused to shiver in silence. Then came the inquest when we met as a Party branch to discuss this seemingly so successful campaign. Our propaganda had very naturally described it as a great success. But what was our verdict at the inquest?

It was that the campaign had been a failure. Why? We had demonstrated to the authorities, and to ourselves, that the housewives of our town were angry at a situation which had grown out of the war. We had had thousands of angry housewives in fighting mood. Then victory had come. But it had come too easily. Now, as a consequence, we had thousands of contented, complacent housewives sitting smugly by their stoves, preening and compliment-ing themselves on what they had achieved by their own efforts. We should have built up class anger; we should have given the campaign a revolutionary content; we ought to have made some converts to the Communist Party, some new readers of the *Daily Worker*. We had not done so. From our point of view the results had been un-helpful rather than helpful to the revolutionary cause. We wrote it off as a failure. That is Bolshevik self-criticism in action.

If there was anything in this for others to adopt and adapt it is surely the attitude of mind. A determination to be absolutely honest with yourself and with each other about what you are doing. To cut through the compli-ments and cant so that it is possible to see whether the

119

purposes of your cause have really been served by the activities in which you have been engaged. To say to yourself and to each other 'What is all this really about, what is it really for?'

*   *   *   *   *

Communists, it is often said, are concerned with changing society, not with changing individual men. This is true in the sense that they believe that they will change men by changing society. That by improving man's environment they will enable him to evolve more rapidly into a fully civilised being. But it is also true to say that the individual Communist is concerned to improve himself and that he can only become a good Communist by doing this. Or, to turn it round the other way, men who are anxious to become better people can find an outlet for this within the Communist Party. This is no doubt one of many reasons why one finds so many former seminarians, spoiled priests, men who in their youth dreamed of being Buddhist monks or Hindu temple priests and still more who, having grown up against a very strong religious family background, have rebelled against their religion yet find a very natural home within the party of atheistic Communism.

The need for the Communist to concern himself with self-improvement is stressed most eloquently and attractively in Liu Shao-chi's *How to be a Good Communist.* This book is based upon a series of lectures delivered at the Institute of Marxism-Leninism in Yenan in 1939 (whilst the Communists were still fighting desperately to achieve their victory), and is studied by Communists the world over no matter whether they be of the pro-Peking or of the pro-Moscow schools.

Liu Shao-chi explains the aims of Communism in global

and heroic terms—as a good Communist instructor should:

'What is the most fundamental and common duty of us Communist Party members? As everybody knows, it is to establish Communism, to transform the present world into a Communist world. Is a Communist world good or not? We all know that it is very good. In such a world there will be no exploiters, oppressors, landlords, capitalists, imperialists or fascists. There will be no oppressed and exploited people, no darkness, ignorance, backwardness, etc. In such a society all human beings will become unselfish and intelligent Communists with a high level of culture and technique. The spirit of mutual assistance and mutual love will prevail among mankind. There will be no such irrational things as mutual deception, mutual antagonism, mutual slaughter and war, etc. Such a society will, of course, be the best, the most beautiful and the most advanced society in the history of mankind. Who will say that such a society is not good? Here the question arises: Can Communist society be brought about? Our answer is "yes". About this the whole theory of Marxism-Leninism offers a scientific explanation that leaves no room for doubt.'

There is a note of almost religious certainty, reminiscent of the early days of Christianity, about that last sentence.

A century ago, Karl Marx told his followers: 'You will have to go through fifteen, twenty, fifty years of civil wars and international conflicts, not only to change the existing conditions, but also to change yourselves and to make yourselves capable of wielding political power.'

Says Liu Shao-chi: 'Thus, men should regard themselves as being in need of, and capable of, being changed. They should not look upon themselves as something unchanging, perfect, holy and beyond reform. It is in no way an insult but the inevitable law of natural and social

121

evolution; otherwise, men cannot make progress. . . .

'To pass from a novice to a mature and well-experienced revolutionary able to cope with any situation calls for a very long process of revolutionary steeling and cultivation, that is, a long process of reformation.'

Marxists see themselves as the conscious and willing instruments of the process of change at work in the world and in human society. Therefore they believe that they can accelerate and direct that process. This is true of their approach to society and of their approach to men, too, particularly their own members.

If they are going to produce a party composed of 'steel-hardened cadres' they must transform the raw material which comes into their hands and do it as effectively as possible. For this reason they pay enormous attention to the task of trying to develop each individual Party member, taking account of varying aptitudes, preferences, talents and potentialities.

Study, Liu Shao-chi observes, can help the process of development. But, he adds: 'We study for the sole purpose of putting into practice what we have learned. It is for the Party and for the victory of the revolution that we study.' The men and women the Party wishes to produce must be an élite.

Membership of the Communist Party has often been likened to membership of a religious order. Those who hold this view will find some support for it in Liu Shao-chi's statement that: 'The Marxist principle is that personal interests must be subordinated to the Party's interests, partial interests to total interests, temporary interests to long-range interests, and the interests of one nation to the interests of the world as a whole.'

Or, again: 'Steeling and cultivation are important for every Party member, whether he be a new member of non-proletarian origin or even a veteran member or a member of proletarian origin. This is because our Communist Party did not drop from the heavens but was born out of Chinese society and because every member of our Party came from this squalid old society. . . . Hence, our Party members have more or less brought with them remnants of the ideology and habits of the old society and they remain in constant association with all the squalid things of the old society. We are still in need of steeling and cultivation in every respect for the sake of enhancing and preserving our purity as the proletarian vanguard and for the sake of raising our social qualities and revolutionary technique.

'That is the reason why Communist Party members must undertake self-cultivation.'

The Christian wrestles with the old Adam, the good Communist wrestles with the old bourgeois beneath the skin.

But the Party member is not left to achieve all that is expected of him in some lonely fight with his baser, bourgeois self. Nor is he left to wrestle alone with his self-cultivation like someone trying to pass some impossibly difficult examinations on the basis of self-study courses. The Party is there to aid him.

In a famous speech to the graduates from the Red Army academies in May 1935, Joseph Stalin launched the slogan: 'Cadres decide everything'. Techniques, he said, were important, but in the final analysis it was upon people that techniques depended for their success. It was no use simply trying to develop techniques if you did not also develop your people.

This slogan was taken up and applied in practical fashion by Communist parties all over the world. In every one of them was established a special Cadres Department. This existed at every level of the Party. Its task was to ensure that each member was developed to the uttermost, made just as effective as possible in the fight for Communism. From the top to the bottom of the Party, at every organisational level, people were appointed to supervise this work.

In a well run local branch, for example, there would be the cadres secretary who was supposed to know all the members individually and to know as much about them as possible. A good cadres secretary kept a card index file in which were noted the forms of activity in which each member engaged, the classes he attended, his response to them, those spheres of activity or study in which he had excelled, those, too, for which he had shown no aptitude or inclination.

Within the particular unit of the Party the cadres secretary had an overriding authority. By this I mean that he was entitled to go to the branch or group leader and say that he considered that Comrade X was being used for too much campaigning, was in danger of becoming an activist who knew little of what all the action was about or, conversely, was attending many classes but doing little of a practical character and so was in danger of becoming an armchair philosopher. He would tell the group leader that this situation had to be rectified, and together they would discuss how the comrade concerned might most easily be persuaded to bring about a proper balance between theory and practice in his life. It would then be the cadres secretary's job to see that this was accomplished.

He would visit a member he considered to be in need of guidance, who looked like developing away from the Party or showed signs of still clinging to old bourgeois prejudices and attitudes. Earnestly they would discuss together how the comrade might improve himself and so become a good Communist, the sort of person he wanted to be.

There is not the slightest doubt that when this cadres work was operating most successfully it brought about the very rapid development of Party cadres, gave the individual Communist a feeling that, having totally committed himself to the Party and submitted himself to the direction of the cadres secretary, he was now an 'improving' person and on the way to perfecting himself as a Communist.

Good 'cadres work' has in the past made a major contribution to the production of the 'men of a special mould' which Stalin said Communists should be. It is the fact that from this relatively small minority group, a quite disproportionate number of leaders has come. They are to be found at the top of trade unions, peasant organisations, professional bodies, cultural groups. It is not all done by trickery. When we seek for explanations we have to look at the training which they have been given, the way in which they have been formed in their study classes, and the way in which the Party develops them from day to day, uses their abilities, draws out their potentialities for self-cultivation and for leadership. And we can admit that all these things the Party does well.

When Stalin concerned himself with the development of people, when he tried to impress upon his Party leaders that people must be treasured and developed, he had of course only a certain section of the people in mind—those in the Communist Party or who were of direct and immediate use to it and, as was later shown, who were of immediate use to himself. His 'humanity' was selective. But his slogan: 'Cadres decide everything' was not a bad one. There is no reason why other people, who are not concerned just to help a minority but with all mankind, should not adapt it to their own purposes.

CHAPTER IX

The Value of Techniques

COMMUNISTS have a deserved reputation for being good propagandists. Again, this does not just happen. It grows out of their whole approach to techniques. It reflects the attitude of mind of this group of people who believe that they have got what the world needs and so have a responsibility to pass it on. Typically, they do not leave it at that. They set about trying to pass it on as efficiently and as effectively as they can.

In trying to gain acceptance of their ideas they meet with a public reaction with which many others are also familiar. People say: 'Well, of course, they can talk all right, but do they do anything?' So they set out to demonstrate that they not only talk but act as well. This naturally makes their propaganda more acceptable to those who become aware of this.

Too often, in my experience, Christians give the impression that they talk, that maybe they have all the right answers too, but then too often do not follow through by putting these into action. The Christian will believe that Communists have the wrong answers, but he will certainly have to acknowledge that they try to put them into practice. The Party know from experience that people tend to be influenced by the mere fact that Communists are not just talking but are doing something, and then go on to accept the thought that they are probably accomplishing something, too.

Communists try to prove to the public that they care about them as people. Anti-Communist propaganda has built up the idea that Communists care only about power. In the newly-developing areas, in particular, they have combated this idea so successfully that there are large numbers of people living in vitally important areas today who, whilst not accepting Communist beliefs or whilst knowing little or nothing about Communist teachings, still believe with absolute conviction that 'only the Communists care'. This is a reflection on Christians and others. It is also a striking tribute to the effectiveness of Communist propaganda. America has contributed immensely more to the development of underdeveloped countries than has the Soviet Union. Christians have done more for those who suffer from poverty and disease than have the Communists. Yet people at the receiving end can still repeat what seems to them to be the self-evident fact that 'only the Communists care'.

This has not been achieved simply on the basis of pouring out more spoken and written words than have come from the rest of the world. Where the Communists' work has been at its best they have given a great deal of thought to the various means by which the public can be convinced the anti-Communist propagandists are wrong when they describe the Communists as mere wordmongers.

In various parts of Asia in recent years, when Communist Party congresses, which bring together all the national and local leaders, have been called, these have been seen as so many opportunities for demonstrating to the public that Communists believe in action on behalf of the people.

The congress meets, not in some big city which can provide the sort of hotel accommodation normally provided for American conventions or British trade union conferences, but in some remote place. One of the greatest needs of areas which are trying to develop is roads, the means of linking isolated villages with highways and with the outside world. Only when a local community is linked up in this way is it likely to begin to advance and to leave behind a pattern of life which may have been unchanged for centuries.

Precisely such areas have on a number of occasions been deliberately chosen by Asian Communist Parties as congress meeting places. Delegates are called together a week before their deliberations are due to begin. During the seven days preceding the opening of the conference the delegates—top leaders and all—work together to build a road which will link the local community to the nearest highway. This ensures that the people will never forget that it was when the Communists came that their development, their possibilities for a better life, began. Any anti-Communist propagandist who goes to them and tells them that Communists 'only talk' is likely to find an unreceptive audience.

Political parties today are very much concerned about creating an image which they hope will be acceptable to the public. Public relations experts and advertising agencies are brought in for the purpose. It is all rather artificial, this attempt to create by slick publicity methods an image which does not necessarily have much relation to the actual performance past, present or potential of the party concerned. Sooner or later the public must sense this. But, when the Communists set out to create an image by the means I have just described, this looks genuine and convincing. It is certainly likely to achieve more among an unsophisticated public than all the costly publicity methods of the Communists' opponents.

This does not mean that the Communists reject the

128

modern propaganda methods. They try to use them and adapt them just as effectively and imaginatively as they can.

Printed Propaganda

When I was working on the *Daily Worker* the paper was both banned and bombed. As a consequence our staff was dispersed. There was a war on, and so some were directed into industry, more into the armed forces—from which, incidentally, most of them emerged in due course as officers. Then, after Russia had been brought into the war, the ban was lifted. Quite suddenly, the one or two of us who were left had to get together a new staff. There was little opportunity to pick and choose, but one thing was essential. That was that they should be intelligent and politically sound. They must be good Communists.

Our new staff consisted of a furrier, engineers, house wives, anyone but trained journalists who at that moment were simply unobtainable. We had to train in journalism this mixed group just as quickly as possible. Our aim was to produce a paper which was competing directly with the best that the millionaire Press could produce, therefore they had to be turned into top grade newspaper people. In addition, we had to make them into good *Communist* journalists. People who would use journalism in order to aid the Communist cause. When I briefed my staff before the first issue of the new paper was produced, I reminded them that Lenin had said that the whole art of Communist journalism is to get profound ideas across in simple language. It was something which I never ceased to hammer away at, for the easiest thing for someone who is writing for a cause is to become turgid, doctrinaire and unreadable.

Admittedly, this is precisely how much of what the

129

DEDICATION AND LEADERSHIP

Communists produce for their own members appears to the outsider. But in this case, those responsible for it are writing for the initiated, the well instructed members who already know the jargon—and every specialised branch of knowledge has its own jargon. But in their propaganda to the non-Communists, the success of Communist journalists and writers may be judged by their ability to get profound ideas across in simple language. They themselves would say that the test of whether they really understand their Marxism lies in whether they are able to convey it to others in simple terms.

These were the principles which we had learned from Lenin and which guided us as we restarted the *Daily Worker*. I might mention in passing that within a very short time it was judged to be the best news-edited tabloid of the year and received an award as such, in direct competition with the millionaire 'capitalist' Press.

Each member of my reporting staff was encouraged to begin his day with a quick reading of the rest of the Press. In particular, he was expected to see his opposite numbers on the other papers as direct rivals and compare their stories with his own. And as he judged whether he or they had done a better job he had to apply to himself a double test. Firstly, his story must be as well written, easily understood and well informed as the best in the capitalist papers. Secondly, it must, if at all possible, have provided the *Daily Worker* reader with a Marxist interpretation of the situation or a Communist guide to action. A Communist paper, said Lenin, must be an educator, an agitator and an organiser for Communism. Around his paper *Iskra* (the *Spark*) he built up the Bolshevik Party, prepared the way to the revolution and set fire to one-sixth of the world. We set out to make our paper an educator, agitator and organiser for Communism, too. It is worth noting in passing that new Communist Parties are being organised all over Black Africa today around a tiny quarterly *The African Communist* in the best Leninist tradition.

All over the newly-developing areas the Communists have succeeded in spreading their basic ideas in the simple language of the people. Often these have spontaneously spread so widely that it is impossible to trace them directly to the Communists; they have launched them on the world and others have taken them up.

For example, when I was touring Northern and Southern Rhodesia some time ago, frequently speaking to exclusively African audiences, in African townships, at public meetings, in colleges, schools and seminaries, I found that Africans there had almost universally accepted two simple, but false, propositions: that Russia is the big brother who helps poor struggling colonial peoples to achieve their freedom, and, that when they have achieved their freedom, Russia and the other Communist countries provide aid without strings.

No Communist Party as such existed in the Federation, as it then was, at the time. A Marxist study group was just beginning to meet in Northern Rhodesia but was still too small and new to be able to claim the responsibility for such a widely held point of view. Yet, even before the Communists had moved in, these ideas, so useful as part of the softening-up process, had already gained credence amongst the majority of the African population. They had reached them by means of many different types of people, through a variety of different channels. In some cases the ideas had been brought by people who had visited the headquarters of the Afro-Asian Solidarity Organisation in Cairo; it is likely that nationalist leaders who had been to Pan-African conferences had picked them up too. Some had been put into circulation by Peking and Moscow Radio. One can find much the same situation in Asia and Latin America. It is a tribute to the effectiveness of the Communists' propaganda.

Anyone concerned either with counter-propaganda or with trying to get our own positive ideas across would do well to study the Communists' methods, in a mood of humility. There is much to be learned from them. Some of what has still to be learned by the West may appear to be almost absurdly simple and elementary, but it is important nonetheless. For example, never to use a long word where a short one will serve equally well, never to write with the idea of proving one's own erudition but rather in order to ensure that one's ideas shall be made as understandable to the reader as possible.

Anyone engaged in trying to get ideas across and who studies the Communists' methods will quickly see that they have learned to use the simplest terms particularly when they are trying to reach simple people. They adapt what they have to teach to the particular audience. This is something which the West has been slow to learn. The 'answer to Communism' which sounds completely convincing to a group of highly-educated people from a sophisticated background, employed in an office in Washington, D.C., or in London will not necessarily sound convincing to the man in the African township or the Asian kampong.

Lenin had good reason to know that simple ideas can send unsophisticated people into action. They may seem elementary, almost laughably so, to others, yet simple men will die for them.

One recalls the story told by a journalist who was in Petrograd at the time of the Bolshevik Revolution. The counter-revolution was just beginning. Somewhere, out beyond the outskirts of the city, gunfire could be heard. The journalist, deciding that he should be on the spot to get his story, asked people to direct him to the Front. It took him a long time to find anyone who had any idea where it was. Then he saw a truckload of peasants bumping across a frozen ploughed field who told him that they were going to try and find the Front so that they could join in the fighting in defence of the Revolution. They invited him to accompany them. He clambered up into the truck and found that they were sitting on a rolling cargo of hand-grenades.

Journalist-fashion, he started to interview them. He reminded them—although they needed no reminding—that they were probably going to die. They accepted this as obviously the case. He asked them what they were going to die for. He put his question to one after the other. And one after the other they fumbled with their words, too illiterate, too inarticulate after generations of serfdom, to be able to put into words what they wanted to say.

At last, he found one who haltingly explained. 'You see, comrade,' he said, 'all through history there have been two classes, the rich and the poor, and the poor have always been trodden down by the rich. We are poor. We belong to the class which has always been exploited. Now, at last, the poor are coming into their own and are going to build a society in which there will be no more poverty. That is what we are prepared to die for.'

It is for such simple ideas that men will die. Not one of those peasants could have explained even the rudiments of dialectical materialism. In all probability none had ever heard of it. The name of Lenin, as the champion of the poor, was known to them, but they were illiterate and so had never read his writings. But Lenin and his fellow Bolsheviks had succeeded in reducing their message to a simple proposition for simple people. In so doing they made a major contribution to the victory of the revolution. For revolutions, no matter whether they are bloody Communist ones or peaceful Christian ones, are made by simple people, even though they may be led by intellectuals.

If a Communist who is put on to propaganda work has been a good Communist he will already be close to the people. He will know their language, the way they think, the way they express their ideas. It is therefore easy for him to do his propaganda in their language, to know what will get through to them and what will not. The spokesmen of the non-Communist world too often are remote from the minds and lives of those to whom they wish to convey ideas.

The Communists would say that, if your propaganda is to succeed, then you cannot live sealed off from the world. You must identify yourself with those amongst whom you wish to do your propaganda. The burden is on you. You have to find a way to get your ideas to them. If they are not receptive, it is no good blaming them. It is because you have not found a way to make them receptive. You will only do this if you understand how their minds work and if you make what is meaningful to them immensely meaningful to yourself.

Stalin once wrote: 'I think that the Bolsheviks remind us of the hero of Greek mythology, Antaeus. They, like Antaeus, are strong because they maintain connection with their mother, the masses, who gave birth to them, suckled them and reared them. And as long as they maintain connection with their mother, with the people, they have every chance of remaining invincible.

'That is the clue to the invincibility of Bolshevik leadership.'

Or, as *The History of the Communist Party of the Soviet Union* puts it: 'A party perishes if it shuts itself up in its narrow party shell, if it severs itself from the masses. . . .'

I recall a conversation I once had with a priest in Korea who was deploring the fact that, although, at last, educated Koreans were beginning to come to what had previously been exclusively the church of the poor, there was no literature to be offered them in their own language. The best available were a dozen or so poorly translated and excessively sugary, pious books and pamphlets, most of them lives of saints. There was nothing to appeal to the intellectual in his own tongue. The priest went on to explain that it was 'big face' for a Korean writer to sprinkle quotations from the Chinese classics liberally throughout his writings—in order to prove his own erudition. The trouble was that this made what he wrote just about as meaningful to the average reader as would be a British tabloid paper filled with Greek or Latin quotations. And so, time after time, the Catholic authorities had rejected the literary efforts of their own Korean writers. 'We simply cannot get them to write in the simple language of the people,' he said.

I asked him if this was characteristic of all Koreans. To this he replied: 'I would have said so until the Communists came in from North Korea and flooded the country with pamphlets and leaflets which were written in the language of the people. There were no quotations from classical Chinese in them. They found the means of getting their ideas across in simple language whilst our own people were still preoccupied with big face, which is a form of pride. The Communists were not concerned about making a big impression, their concern was to spread Communism.'

The principle that the Communist must be 'the best man at his job' pays rich dividends with the printed word. It is not a coincidence that some of the best colour printing in the world comes from Communist China and East Germany. When the Communist countries want to pump their propaganda into literature-hungry areas, where there is an undiscriminating public, they will be most concerned about getting simple ideas over in simple language, rather

135

than with the quality of the paper on which these are printed or with the artistic merits of the type and layout. But, when they are directing the printed word to a public which can appreciate something good, they aim to make it the best.

It was this approach to propaganda that the Communists of Italy brought to their tremendous poster campaigns which were such a feature of Italian elections in the first postwar years. Some of the posters were amongst the best produced anywhere. There was something for everyone. They were aimed at every level.

Catholics saw this as a challenge. The Civic Committees, under the wing of Catholic Action, produced first-rate posters too. To them the 1948 elections were of decisive importance and so they virtually threw aside all pretence at being non-political. They brought the same approach to the poster campaign as did the Communists. They found the very best amongst Catholics employed in Press and publicity, poster artists, commercial artists, journalists, publicists and advertising experts. The Communists would go to a city and plaster every wall with wonderfully ingenious, often wickedly satirical, posters. Within a few hours the local Civic Committee members were going around pasting up others which either directly debunked those of the Communists' or provided an answer to them. They were careful to see that they were just as good in design, just as imaginative, as amusing, as devastating. Poster for poster, they were as good as the Communists' best. This contest captured the imagination of the Italian public and the world's press, too, who called it the 'Battle of the Posters'. It played a significant part in winning those decisive elections, and keeping Communism at bay. But this is exceptional. Too often, if and when a reply to the Communist propaganda comes from a non-Communist, it has the look of being inferior to theirs.

136

Films and Discs

The Communists bring this same approach to the making of films. Every little mission congregation, every little religious order wants to have its film today. Too often it is felt to be an exceptional achievement to have produced a film at all and the results make this painfully apparent. The most faithful of the order's followers go along to see the film despite its inferiority. But because it is substandard it is unlikely to reach out beyond the converted to the unconverted. In other words, it fails in what is, presumably, its true purpose.

I can remember going, at the end of a hunger march in the early 1930s to see a film put on by the Communist Party. The film we were shown was Eisenstein's *Battleship Potemkin*. It had been reduced to 16 mm., but it was still superb. Its powerful, revolutionary propaganda got across. The then recent Invergordon Mutiny of a section of the British fleet, in which Communists played a leading role, gave it topicality. The mutiny of the Russian sailors of the battleship *Potemkin* had a message for an audience which was already in conflict with the Establishment. But the message got home immensely more powerfully and vividly because of the techniques which Eisenstein had employed—because it came as near to technical perfection as was possible at that time.

The propaganda need not necessarily be direct, it need not be obvious propaganda at all, in order to be effective. One of the most successful pieces of atheist Communist propaganda I ever saw was a nature film, not a political one. Those who made it resisted the temptation either to put any politics into it or to include a single word of open propaganda. The camera work was excellent. The colours convincing.

The film had been made in rural Hungary. First, you

137

went hunting with a polecat. You followed it into a rabbit hole and saw it kill baby rabbits whilst their mother, in a simple sequence shot full of natural tension and drama, tried to defend them. You followed the little beast of prey as it went from one bird's nest to the next, driving off parent birds, then sucking their eggs or killing their young.

Next you hunted with an eagle high in the sky. Again, the photography was breath-takingly good, and well nigh inexplicable to the layman. With the eagle, you hovered over some smaller bird, then swept down with it to the kill. And all the time the scenery below was magnificent.

Finally, by means of underwater photography, you hunted with fishes. You saw big fish swallowing innumerable smaller ones, or, without waiting for them to begin life, devouring the fishes' eggs even as they were laid by the female. That was all.

It was, I repeat, the best Communist atheist propaganda film I ever saw. One could imagine what happened as it was taken around from one Hungarian village hall to the next. Everyone would go to see it. Here was something that was close to the lives of country people, of people who work on the soil, for whom birds, animals and fish are part of their lives. This was their language, their world.

The peasants who saw the film would surely marvel at what they were shown. Then, on the following day, on the collective farm or the co-operative, the Communist amongst them would ask if they had been to the village hall last night to see the nature film, and what did they think of it? When he had got general assent as to its excellence and its interest, he would follow through with: 'I will tell you what worried me afterwards, when I got back home and thought about it. Did you notice that the polecat, the eagle and even the fish live by killing others? There was no other way in which they could survive, since this is the way they are made. Of course, that is what the

138

world is like. Now, you, and you, and you who are Catholics, tell me, how a God of love could make a world like that and how you explain this to yourself.'

The average peasant would certainly have great difficulty in finding the answers. So would a great many other people besides. And that was all that was needed to sow the seeds of doubt. It was, I repeat, a superbly done piece of propaganda. It was good technically, close to the lives of the people, it spoke in their language. Then, provided that a Communist came with the 'correct' follow-through, its effect could be deadly.

Once, some years ago, when I was in South Vietnam, I had intended to buy some gramophone records of genuine Vietnamese folk music to add to my collection. As it worked out, I had to leave Saigon in a hurry and before any records could be bought. Some time later I was in Paris where some Vietnamese friends were my hosts. I told them of my disappointment at not having been able to get the records I had wanted when I was in their country. They informed me that it was possible to get such discs in Paris. A great many French soldiers had fought in Indo-China. These provided a natural market for them and, in addition, thousands of Vietnamese students lived in and around Paris too. They said that they would take me to a music shop where I could get what I wanted. I reminded them that the type of record I required must be authentic. I wanted nothing that had been jazzed up for a French public. The instruments, the music and the voices must be the genuine thing.

We went together to a music store where an assistant produced a pile of perhaps one dozen records. My host, after rejecting one after the other from the large pile, took just one that satisfied him. 'This one,' he said, 'is the only one which is authentic.' I took it and then, when we had left the shop, I asked why was this the only one which was

139

worth buying. My host confirmed with me that I did not understand the Vietnamese language. Then he explained that all the rest had been Americanised, or Westernised. This, of all the pile, was the only one which met my requirements. There was just one way in which it was not authentic, but, since I did not understand Vietnamese, this would not matter. Technically it was perfect. But, whereas the others came from South Vietnam, this came from the Communist North. The words were Communist propaganda.

And so, he explained, when Vietnamese students sat around, relaxing together on a Saturday night, dreaming and talking of home, in a nostalgic, receptive mood, this was the record, the only authentic one, which they played over and over again. And as a consequence, for the following week they were likely to go around singing its revolutionary words to themselves. The Communists' message would be going continuously through their minds. That is good propaganda. But why blame the Communists for their cunning whilst we degrade a people's culture, insult their national feelings and offer them the second best which we have already conditioned our own public to accept?

Many people in the underdeveloped countries resent the way in which their local cultures are being thus degraded by Americanisation and Europeanisation. They deplore the sight of their own youngsters responding to that same process as is made manifest in their clothes, their speech, their taste for a juke-box culture which is just about all they know of our vaunted Western 'way of life'.

One of the first acts of the new Left-wing government, when Singapore was given self-government, was to start an all-out attack upon 'yellow culture' (degraded Western culture). The near-pornographic Hollywood posters were taken down from the hoardings at the side of the streets, the films they advertised were banished, the pulp literature from the West—paperbacks with lurid covers—were banned from the bookstalls. The brothels were closed. New and stricter regulations were enforced in the hotels. One Chinese Singapurian pagan put it searingly and unforgettably: 'We had to clean up the mess the Christians left behind.'

Hollywood is part of a free enterprise society, part of the price we pay for it. Pulp literature, it seems, is part of the cost of democratic freedom too. But they are bad propaganda and, understandably, this is something upon which the Communists have seized. But they also know what is good propaganda.

The Spoken Word

When the Communist is trained in public speaking, he is told always to keep close to the lives of the people in the examples and anecdotes he uses. Each time he makes a theoretical point, he should illuminate it with a story from the fields, the workshops or the streets, from the working life and interests of the masses. In the Communist Party's early days, their propaganda was what they now describe as 'sectarian'. In other words, they did not care whom they offended. They made no effort to make their ideas acceptable to others. Marxism is, in fact, in conflict with every other philosophy, every other point of view, and the Communist propagandist went into battle every time he mounted the platform. He attacked the beliefs of his hearers, ridiculed their religion, told them that they were spoonfed and dumb. That way, he made enemies, not friends.

Had the Communists continued along that course they would have remained a small unsuccessful group of plotters and no more. As time went on, however, they

141

learned that a more subtle approach was required. This realisation came under the impact of the devastating defeat of the immensely powerful German Communist Party and the triumph of its arch-enemy, Hitler. From that moment the Communists of the non-Communist world realised that they could not afford to go on making enemies quite unnecessarily. What they needed was allies. They needed friends—and to increase their own numbers, too. And so, since then, they have evolved a technique which is just the opposite of the earlier one. Instead of setting out to prove that the other man is wrong, they seek to find a point of contact with his mind, then try to extend the area of sympathetic interest and agreement just as far as possible.

There is no question of non-Communists being able to use the deceits employed by the Communists in their propaganda and in their relations with others. But here is a perfectly good technique. There is nothing immoral in it, nothing that others may not copy.

It is, in the majority of cases, the element of truth, no matter how small it may be, which makes it possible for the Communists to get acceptance for their point of view. There may only be a grain of truth in a bushel of false-hoods but it is that which they will use in order to get their ideas across. But consider the implications of this. If it is the small element of truth in Communist propaganda which makes it acceptable, then those who believe they have *the* truth have an immense advantage over the Communists. They need only improve their own methods of presentation, their own mastery of techniques, their own attempt to bring theory and practice together in their own lives, to gain acceptance for it.

There are Christians who sneer at the Communists because they have to exploit the little bit of truth they have, whilst the Christians have the whole. They might

142

do better to ask themselves why, with truth on their side, they have nonetheless so often failed where the Communists have succeeded—and in areas which are, in the last analysis, far more the legitimate province of the Christian than of the Communist.

Organisation

All this activity, the Communist believes, must be backed up with the right form of organisation. The Party's organisation, as is well known, is based upon small groups or 'cells'. These are its 'basic units'. Through them the Party does its work at grass-roots level. Or, to change the metaphor, they are Communism's cutting edge. It will be seen, therefore, that this form of organisation is of great importance to the Party.

Much has been written about Communist cells by people who appear to have little idea of how they work. For example, it is often said that every Communist belongs to a cell. This, in a limited sense, is true. But the fact is that a Communist may (and most do) belong to many cells because he is an organised Communist the whole of the time and his varied interests will probably take him into many diverse organisations in every one of which he will be organised.

Consider a hypothetical case. A Communist, shall we say, works in a factory. He is also a member of his appropriate trade union. He has a particular interest in the culture of one of the Communist countries, and he has an interest in music when he has time to indulge in it.

In the first place, he will be a member of his local Party branch which is based upon the neighbourhood in which he lives. If the branch is of any size, he will be put into a street or area cell, one of many which make up the local branch. It is a principle of Communist organisation that, wherever you have three or more Communists, there you have a Communist cell. They are expected to work together in this organised way in the interests of Communism.

If, therefore, in the factory in which he is employed, there are three or more Communist Party members, he will belong to his factory cell. If the Party is strong within the factory, and there are three or more members working in his particular department or workshop, he will then be a member of the departmental or workshop cell. It goes almost without saying, Communists being what they are, that if he goes to work in a factory or in a department where there is only one other Communist then together these two will aim as quickly as possible to make a convert so that they may form a cell and so begin organised Communist Party activity. Before he leaves for home there will normally be a quick meeting of his cell where the successes and failures of the day are discussed.

He belongs to his appropriate trade union and if, in his local branch, there are two or more Communists besides himself they, too, will function as a cell within that union branch. Together they will plan their work within it. In advance of branch meetings they will go through the agenda, deciding which resolutions they are going to support, which oppose and which they will initiate. They will draw up resolutions in advance, decide which member of the cell shall move them or, more ideally, which non-Communist can most easily be persuaded to move the resolution for them. When elections to responsible positions in the branch are pending, they will decide in advance whom they will try to get elected, and who must be replaced. This organised activity brings them returns, as many a trade union has discovered.

If our Party member accepts responsibility in his union at local level he will almost certainly do the job to the best

144

of his ability, and as a consequence his promotion to some higher level of the organisation may be suggested by some well-intentioned non-Communist or, alternatively be engineered by the branch cell. Thus he moves on to the area, district or divisional committee of his union. If there are three Communists on that, they will function as a Communist cell, just as in the lower units of the union.

His interest in the culture of one of the Communist countries takes him into an organisation which exists for promoting friendship with, and interest in, just that country. Quite possibly the majority of its members are non-Communists. But, if there is the required number of Party members amongst the organisation's members—and in this case there will almost certainly be many among them—there will be the inevitable organised cell of which, again, he will be a member.

His interest in music may take him into a folk-song group, a gramophone society, an orchestra. Here, too, the same principle applies. He becomes an organised Communist within it, trying to do a job for the cause. This does not make his interest in music any less real, it just adds extra point and purpose. If he is stupid he will do a crude propaganda inside the music society, forever demanding that more and more Soviet music be played. More probably he will be one of the keenest members of the organisation, who comes up most frequently with good ideas, impresses others with the breadth of his musical interest. But out of the personal relationships he establishes some opportunities for the spread of Communist ideas, maybe even for making converts to the cause. If ever, incidentally, the Communist Party should be banned and is therefore driven underground, this last cell may become for the time being the most important to which he belongs.

This, quite obviously, is a form of organisation which only a few non-Communist bodies could, or even would want to, imitate. It is the organisation of an élite, suitable for a body of determined activists with well-defined aims, a single mind and purpose.

But—and this is typical of so much of those aspects of the life of the Communist Party which we have examined —it is the attitude, the approach to the cause, which is of greatest significance and may most profitably be imitated. The Communist is a Communist the whole of the time. By his life and example he challenges the Christian to become integrated and to be a Christian the whole of the time.

An oft-told story concerns General Booth, founder of the Salvation Army, who, when asked why it was that the Army set its hymns to popular current tunes, replied: 'I see no reason why the Devil should have all the best tunes.'

There would appear to be no reason why the Devil should be allowed to have all the best techniques either.

CHAPTER X

Leaders for What?

Lenin said he wanted a party of what he called 'professional revolutionaries'. He did not mean by this that they would be paid. They were to be professional in the sense that they would not be amateurs, that their methods would not be amateurish. They would fight for Communism as though they were fighting a war. They would fight like a disciplined army, sweeping away the existent society as a necessary precondition for building the new one.

And so the Communist Party all over the world, modelled on Lenin's original Russian pattern, sets out to make itself an organisation of professional revolutionaries. People who live for the revolution from the moment they get up in the morning to the time they go to bed at night. As trained and disciplined people.

International Communism's inner Party journal, *The World Marxist Review,* frequently refers to Communists as 'soldiers of the revolution'. This is how they see themselves. And the fight goes on, no matter whether they are operating in a 'revolutionary situation', or in periods of more gradual change, which they see as ones of preparation. In that situation, they set out to establish themselves as leaders. They cannot all be leaders of the Communist Party itself, for it would be a case of all chiefs and no

Indians. That is not the aim. Each Communist Party member is expected to be a leader in any field of activity into which life may take him. Trained automatically, spontaneously to take up a position of leadership wherever he goes. After all, men are not suddenly going to follow the Communists, when at last the barricades go up in the streets, unless they have already established themselves as leaders. Stalin, at the grave of Lenin, said: 'We Bolsheviks are men of a special mould.' The Communist Party everywhere sets out to produce men of a special mould. I hope that by now we have seen that it succeeds in this. That is what justifies our present study.

The man moulded by Communism, the new Marxist man, is a very formidable one. He is cast in the opposite mould to the New Man in Christ. Even though his original motivation may have been generous, even though he retains much of his initial idealism and sense of oneness with suffering humanity, still, because he has accepted an evil creed, his life tends to become evil too. So the mould into which the Communist is pressed is one that ultimately debases him as a man—and this is particularly true where Communism has already come to power.

Part of the tragedy of Communism is that it takes good men, with good intentions, and uses them for a bad cause. Because its approaches to God, to the nature of man and to the world, are false, it starts off on the wrong foot. The consequence is that the idealists, and natural rebels who join the Communist Party, set out to be the saviours of mankind and become instead men's jailers. Communism stands condemned, not only for what it does to the masses, but also for what it does to the Communists themselves.

Nonetheless, as I have tried to show, it is true to say that the Communists display an impressive belief in the individuals who make up the Communist movement. Their sense of dedication, their idealism, is constantly fed

148

and maintained by the Party itself. Some of this is the result of good organisation and careful planning, some the result of the formation, training and 'cadres work' to which the Party has devoted so much time and thought.

The conversion of a man into a 'steel-hardened cadre' does not necessarily destroy his idealism. Most often, side by side with the instruction and formation, the hardening process, still goes the original warm idealism because this is something to which Communism never hesitates, nor ceases, to appeal. I have indicated that this is not something peculiar to Western Communists. There is abundant evidence to show that this is so.

I remember some years ago talking to a man from Indo-China who had fought with the Communists at the great siege of Dien Bien-Phu. I met him at Hong Kong. He was a Catholic from North Vietnam who had been conscripted into Ho Chi Minh's army.

Our Western Press had been full of the glory of the French army which had put up such tremendous resistance, at what was to prove to be its last ditch stand against the Communist-led assault. The French held on to the fortress for weeks on end, enduring all the immense suffering that a protracted siege entails.

We did not, however, hear much about the men and the experiences on the other side. How about the people who were fighting against the French? Besieging a fortress is a difficult and bloody business too. I asked my Catholic from North Vietnam: 'What sort of briefing did they give you before they sent you into action?'

The briefing they were given was this: 'You will almost certainly die. Already, even to get within gun range, you have to clamber and slither over men's rotting bodies, the bodies of your own comrades. The probability is that you will die, just as they have done. If you do, you will not

149

just be dying in the fight against French colonialism. You will not just be dying for Vietnam. You will be dying for suffering, oppressed humanity all over the world. Your death will help to make the world a better place.'

Now that was the briefing which atheist leaders gave to their followers before they went into action. They were not afraid to call upon them to die and they did not hesitate to base this upon an appeal to the idealism which is deep in the heart of every man. They demonstrated, as Communists have so often done, that this is a powerful thing. And their followers went into action, wave upon wave, ready to die so that others might live. They were sent into battle morally prepared for the fight.

The Communist Parties of Latin America believe they have a period of exceptional promise before them, opportunities such as they never had before. But the leaders also believe that before they can reach their goal, almost certainly for every one of them and for most of their followers, there must be another period of illegality, of suffering, of jailings, torture and possibly martyrdom. They do not hesitate to contemplate such a period, or to prepare for it either. Nor, again, do they hesitate to tell their followers what lies ahead.

Most of the Communist Parties of Latin America have already lived through periods of illegality and, in many cases, through several such periods. They know from hard experience what is involved. There are many Communist leaders in Latin America today who have spent as many as eighteen out of the last twenty-five years in prison. Many of them bear on their flesh the signs of tortures which they have suffered in the prisons of their opponents. The Communist Party of Venezuela is one which spent years as an outlawed party and has only recently known what it is to be able to operate more or less freely above ground.

Yet even now it is preparing itself for another period of illegality. More than this, it is actually looking forward to it in the sense that it believes that this will provide the opportunity for a showdown.

Some time ago, as part of its preparation for this, it produced a document which was circulated amongst its own members and then later among Communists in other parts of Latin America. Its purpose was to prepare them for the coming period of illegality.

It takes the form of a history of the Party. Since much of that history has been lived in underground conditions it becomes quite naturally a manual for underground workers. It is written in such a way as, not only to record what was done in the past, but to prepare and arm its members for what the future holds. Let me give you one or two examples from it:

'Party members must keep party secrets and safeguard the organisation and leaders. Conceit, carelessness, mistakes which are likely to prejudice the security of the Party organisation cannot be tolerated. Great harm can also be caused by treacherous people who are easily taken in or who fall for the police bait. Informers and those who yield under police torture merit the contempt of the Party. There can be no excuse here. Joining the Communist Party, every revolutionary should be aware that he may be arrested, become a victim of the enemy's attack. It is, therefore, important for him to be prepared politically and morally to endure these trials with honour. . . .

'Having fallen into the enemy's hands, the Communist should realise that he is now on a new battlefield. His imprisonment is not a matter of his personal life, but part of the class struggle, a political event, a blow at the Party. He must fight might and main on this new front, in order to be useful to the cause of the Party and the revolution,

151

When in jail, he must knit together the arrested revolutionaries, keep up their morale and revolutionary vigilance, help the less experienced comrades, correct those who commit errors or who act imprudently. The main thing is to be firm. A moment of weakness may disgrace the revolutionary for ever. A moment of cowardice may cancel out years of devoted service to the working class. Neither torture nor lack of experience, state of health, or any other reason can justify betrayal of the cause of the Party.'

That is the briefing which Latin American Communists are receiving at this moment. It is a preparation for deliberately going into a period of illegality, imprisonment, if necessary torture. This is what I mean when I talk of Communists feeling themselves to be soldiers of the revolution. A member of the Communist Party can be made to feel that it is almost an honour to be faced with such a challenge, such an opportunity.

They, of course, believe that they will see the realisation of their goal of a Communist world or, at any rate, will see the world launched on the way to that goal, in this period in which we live. Lenin said that this is 'the epoch of the proletarian revolution and the proletarian dictatorship'. And that, many may say, highlights one of the vast number of differences between Communism and Christianity. Communism is new, Christianity is old. More than this, it is old and tired. Over a period of nearly 2,000 years, something has got lost somewhere along the line. Communists, like the early Christians, are most of them converts. The mass of the Catholic community and of other Christian communities are 'born' Christians.

Yet this is not really so. Each generation in turn must be evangelised anew. Each generation of young people coming along must be Christianised all over again. That, of course, has been true throughout the centuries.

152

It is true in a particular sense today for we are now at the beginning of a process of renewal. That is one reason why the Second Vatican Council has been looking back to the early centuries. This is understandable, because this is looking back to a period before so many barnacles had accumulated on the bottom of St. Peter's barque. When the 'people of God' were less stratified, as between hierarchy, clergy and laity than they are now. When communication between them was spontaneous and real. But the Church is also looking to the twentieth and for that matter, to the twenty-first centuries, too.

Almost the only thing that is certain about the period which lies ahead of us is that it will be a period of great change. This is a process that has already started and there can be no stopping it. The process is likely to be accelerated, rather than slowed down.

The society in which the Christian must operate, in which he feels himself called upon to lead, will not be as it is now. We have no reason to wish it to be. There never was anything to back up the talk, so fashionable a few years ago, of the 'atheist East' and the 'Christian West'. The leaders of the East, if by this is meant, in defiance of all geography, the Communist-ruled countries, were atheist, as they still are. The society they are building is constructed on atheistic foundations. They practise what they preach and so they are trying to build a society without God.

But there never was anything much more than wishful thinking to justify the label of the 'Christian West'. The cause of religion is not served by using 'free enterprise society' and 'Christianity' as though they were interchangeable and synonymous terms. The free enterprise society may be affluent—for some—and it has certainly achieved higher material standards than men have ever before known. This does not make it more Christian. Indeed, the evidence suggests that it is more likely to have the reverse effect. There is nothing in Christian social teaching to support the widely held view that men have an inalienable human right to an ever-rising standard of life regardless of what is happening to other men in the neighbouring borough, on the other side of the tracks, or on the other side of the world.

Here is still quite clearly a very big job for Christians to do, a tremendous fight into which they can throw themselves along with people of other religions, and, for that matter, along with secular humanists and other men of goodwill—to make an end of the present scandal where, as one part of the world gets richer, the other quite literally gets poorer. The gap widens between the rich nations and the poor nations, between the prosperous north and the poverty-stricken south.

According to the United Nations Food and Agriculture Organisation there is more hunger in the world today than there was in 1945. This, despite the fact that ours is the first generation in the whole history of man which has the scientific and technological means to make an end of hunger. We are morally involved in this problem as men never were before. Yet, despite this, Christians sleep peacefully in their beds at night, with easy consciences.

There can be no doubt that here is as big a job to do, as great a challenge as ever the early Christians had to face. There is just as much reason why the Christian should want to go into battle against these evil things as there is for a Communist soldier of the revolution to enter his own particular fight. Capitalist society has shown itself to be immensely adaptable. Whatever may be said for or against capitalism this, at any rate, can be said in its favour: it has shown itself capable of fundamental change. The very bases of capitalism today are unlike those of

Marx's day. Then it was based upon small enterprises in fierce competition with each other. Today it is based on huge monopolies who reduce genuine competition to a minimum. If it has changed once, it can be changed again. If the Christian believes that it would be the better for being more Christian, he has a right and a duty to try to make it so. If he believes that it should be transformed, then there is every reason why he should set about the task of trying to Christianise himself, and simultaneously trying to make the society in which he lives one in which the human personality can develop, into a society which no longer degrades men and makes it virtually impossible for any of them to live a decent life.

If the Communist, therefore, has a reason to want to spread his Communism, so, too, has the Christian. The Christian will do well to take a leaf out of the Communist book and to recognise that nothing is gained by squandering our human material or letting it go to waste, as is so often the case today. Everything is to be gained by using it well. If one really is setting out to do a job, then it is only commonsense to make it as effective as possible. If you believe that, say, public opinion needs to be rescued from present trends, then there is every reason why also you should try to make the Christian impact upon it as great as possible.

For this task, dedicated Christian leaders will be needed. There are techniques which can be learned and there is every reason why they should be studied, then taught to others.

We have been taking a very selective look at Communism in action, as I warned right at the start, we would do. I have not been looking for the evil in it, not pinpointing what is false in its teaching or dishonest in its practice. The purpose of this operation has been to look at the Communists, this extremely successful minority, to see

155

what we have to learn from them. We have seen that they are not just so many thugs and crooks. They are good, not bad, human material. We have looked at some of the methods they use and have found effective. Some of these we may possibly be able to imitate, some are capable of adaptation, in the case of others our ideas may spark off theirs, precisely because only the very opposite of what they do is open to us. But any examination of their methods, their formation and use of people must be challenging.

I suppose the fight for what is good has always to take two forms, the fight for truth and the fight against falsehood. In this study, we have been concentrating on the positive side of the fight, almost to the exclusion of the other. For myself, I would feel that we need more Christian leaders as an answer to the trained Communist leaders. We shall most effectively provide answers to Communism, not by producing more militant, purely negative anti-Communists, certainly not by producing more amateur detectives, but by producing more educated, adult democrats and, more particularly, more well-instructed, dedicated, totally committed religious believers.

Nonetheless, it is true to say that there is no part of the world today where the Communists are not active; and, more or less inevitably, those who believe Communism to be a disastrously false doctrine and, even more, those who have to live under it, must oppose its spread. It may seem an unrewarding fight, a fight not of our choice, but at times it is a very necessary one.

The task of making leaders is really one of creating an attitude of mind. When some new situation arises, the reaction of most people is to ask; when is someone going to do something about it? The spontaneous reaction of the trained leader is at once to ask himself: what do I do in this situation?

He comes before his fellows and says: We should do this and that and the other. And they follow him. Partly because he speaks with authority, they respect him and look up to him, but also because they have learned from experience that he has something to offer.

The Communist is taught always to ask himself: What do I do as a Communist? The answer he provides flows direct from his beliefs. Action and belief are always related in his mind and in his practice too.

The Christian, if he is going to match the Communist man for man, might profitably ask: What do I do as a Christian? Then act accordingly. Something in the nature of a social revolution and a moral regeneration would occur in the life of the West if every committed Christian we already have were to acquire, or to be given, this attitude of mind and start to think in these terms.

In practice one learns to lead by leading—provided that one has been suitably prepared and trained to learn from one's mistakes.

The Communists are not interested in producing leaders as such. It is Communist leaders they want. Men who will lead for the cause not just for themselves. The same surely goes for Christians too. Our public and professional life is full of people who are leaders who are also Christians. The purpose of Christian leadership training is not just to help ambitious men to the top, or to make little men who have done leadership courses feel bigger than they really are. Still less is it to produce führers, either large or small.

It has much more to do with the making of integrated people. Ones who understand what they believe, are deeply dedicated to it, and who try unceasingly to relate their beliefs to every facet of their own lives and to the society in which they live.

To the Christian there is something peculiarly poignant

157

about atheist Communists saying, as so many so often do, from the very depths of their hearts, 'There is nothing too good for the Party' and then going out and making their actions match their words. There is no need to underline what the Christians' positive response to that should be.